Wellbeing Economics

Wellbeing Economics

How and Why Economics Needs to Change

Nicky Pouw

Amsterdam University Press

Also published as *Welzijnseconomie: Hoe en waarom de economie moet veranderen.*
ISBN: 978 94 6372 660 3

Translation to English: Vivien Collingwood

Cover illustration: designed by Jamilla van der Werff, 2020
Cover design: Gijs Mathijs Ontwerpers, Amsterdam
Lay-out: Crius Group, Hulshout

ISBN	978 94 6372 385 5
e-ISBN	978 90 4855 358 7 (ePub)
DOI	10.5117/9789463723855
NUR	780

To Lulu, Eva and Rosa – my reasons for living well

Table of Contents

List of figures and tables

Foreword

Allister McGregor

The discipline of economics has had a vital role to play in the development of our societies and in improvements in the human condition. Since its formal invention as a social science in the 18th Century, it has shaped how we organize production, conduct exchange and arrange for the distribution of goods and services. Some commentators are positive about how it has helped to lift many human beings out of poverty and penury, (for example, the enthusiastic Hans Rosling), while others have been longstanding critics of its complicity in the colonial and post-colonial subjugation of some countries and regions to the needs of others. But, no matter what good it has contributed in the past, it is now a discipline that is in deep trouble. The orthodoxy of modern economics is profoundly implicated in many of the major problems that the world currently faces: the persistence of widespread and harmful poverty, the growth of extreme inequality; and increasing levels of environmental degradation. While it may have been a discipline that was suited to the needs of a particular era in human history, and to a particular period of political (in)sensitivity, in its orthodox form it is now no longer fit for purpose.

The acceleration of globalisation has been fed by and has hyped the spread of orthodox neo-classical economics. It has become, as Foucault has contended, an essential component of contemporary global governmentality. While it was once a rounded social science, accommodating a range of views and exploring complex understandings of how economics interplays with politics and societal organization, modern orthodox economics has lost touch with its social aspect and with the human beings that it was intended to serve. Moreover, since the 1980s, it has transformed more into an ideology than a science. It no longer just provides the tools to solve problems, it seeks to tell us what the values are that people should live by; what is rational and what is not; and it presents us with one set of policy solutions as the only credible ones for governments to adopt.

In 1992, Frances Fukayama proclaimed that the dissolution of the Soviet Union marked the 'end of history', he might equally have been talking about the discipline of economics. Prior to the neo-classical economics revolution of the 1980s, Departments of Economics taught a broad range of topics ranging from the history of economic thought to non-orthodox approaches to economics. This has largely come to an end and Departments of Economics now tend to teach a toxic combination of mathematics and neo-classical dogma. It has become increasingly apparent to many young people coming through as students eager to understand the problems of the world and find solutions to them that economics needs to be thoroughly rethought and recast as a social science.

In this book Nicky Pouw makes a valuable contribution to this process of reimagining economics. Building on work that she and I undertook earlier she argues that the first and fundamental step is that economics must refocus on human wellbeing. It is by putting real human beings back at the centre of the discipline that many of the shortcomings of the current orthodoxy can be addressed. This is a no superficial call to 'bring humans back to the centre of our analysis', it is a step that has major ontological, epistemological and methodological ramifications for the discipline. The book does not shy away from these difficult issues but rather offers a thorough review of how this new focus on human wellbeing changes key axioms, ideas and approaches to study. Not least it deals with issues of the interaction of humans with the natural environment; the problems of growing inequality; the undervaluing of women's work; and the disastrous problem of how care is not valued or is unvalued in orthodox economics. The book also addresses the issue of economics as ideology and makes a strong appeal for the return to pluralism in the discipline of economics. After all, if people can hold different values and different cultures have a legitimate claim to distinctive ways of addressing societal issues, then modern economics cannot be a mono-cultural leviathan.

The book represents an excellent starting point as a teaching resource for students wishing to break away from the orthodoxy. It provides very helpful illustrations of issues that use real people as the point of reference and not some idealized cypher. Seeking to change the discipline of modern economics is a difficult task, as the orthodoxy is well entrenched and its ideas are hardwired into the thinking of many academics, teachers and policy-makers. Unfortunately, one aspect of the evolution of economics into an ideology is that many of the proponents of neo-classical economics become brainwashed by their own axioms and assumptions about human nature. The model makes the reality. The assumptions about *homo economicus* (who is, by the way, a white middle-aged bloke, who has a good level of income and wealth, who lives in an ordered, disaster-proof society, and who is confident in his position of power) causes some people to try to emulate him: to behave as self-interested, maximising agents who pursue efficiency and profit at all costs in the belief that if we were all to behave in this way we would have better societies. This is not the case however and that is the road to an asocial dystopia. The recent corona virous pandemic has demonstrated that when confronted by an unprecedented disruptive challenge, then market based arrangements break down and it is only the humanity and sociability of human beings that can begin to provide appropriate responses. It is the neighbours assisting the vulnerable in their communities; it is the health workers working excessive hours in difficult conditions to take care of the sick; it is only the care-workers putting themselves at risk to care for the elderly or infirm. It is these very human efforts that have enabled many communities and societies to meet and overcome the challenge. It is this that demonstrates that we should seize this opportunity to reshape economics, focusing how we might improve the wellbeing of all humans.

Professor J. Allister McGregor
Associate Fellow, Institute of Policy Research, University of Bath

Acknowledgments

When I travelled in rural Africa for the first time, researching poverty and inequality, I soon became aware of the inestimable value of social capital. In a small village community in Northern Uganda, I had just finished holding a survey on daily eating patterns in rural households. As I was saying goodbye, the woman with whom I had been speaking, who was aged around sixty and single, gave me two eggs. As I knew that she and her family often went hungry, this was an extremely valuable gift. I was astonished, but the team's Ugandan researchers explained that as well as being grateful for our visit, the woman was creating a bond with us; our visit had given her a sense of prestige and status that she must have lacked in her community. Due to the deep poverty in which she lived, she had become virtually invisible to many people. The visit was a certain acknowledgement of her existence; we saw her, and therefore she mattered. A friendship arose between us, and we continued to stop by on a regular basis. We shared family stories and exchanged recipes. We also discussed her situation with the village chief and other members of the community. Slowly, more and more people began to show concern for her. Through our research team she made contact with others from the village and beyond, who came to buy eggs and vegetables from her. With this income, she was able to buy new clothes and make small improvements to her home. She also invested in more chickens and built a small chicken run. All of this strengthened her self-confidence, she later told me. She went out more often, and started to participate in village festivities and meetings again. What began as an exchange of information grew into in a friendship, one that conferred mutual recognition and access to a wider social and economic network. The value of social capital is difficult to express in monetary terms, but it is closely interwoven with our wellbeing as humans. Ultimately, this is likely to have been more valuable than the two eggs, although it is impossible to demonstrate this objectively at a particular moment in time. What we can say, though, is that a form of initial 'exchange' took place between the woman and myself: two eggs in exchange for information. This initial exchange eventually brought us more than either had anticipated; something that contributed to our wellbeing, with unexpected side-effects on other scale levels.

I would not have been able to write this book without the opportunity I received from my research group, Governance and Inclusive Development (GID) at the Department of Geography, Planning and Development Studies at the University of Amsterdam (UvA), particularly Joyeeta Gupta and Jochem de Vries. Although the prevailing trend today is to publish articles, they gave me the time and freedom to work on a 'slow' project such as this book. I am grateful to be able to work in the multidisciplinary research environment of the Amsterdam Institute of Social Science Research, led by Brian Burgoon. My colleagues in the GID group stimulate me every day with their non-economic research on global poverty, inequality and development in various contexts: Joyeeta Gupta, Isa Baud, Maarten Bavinck, Mirjam-Ros Tonen, Hebe Verrest, Mieke Lopes Cardozo, Esther Miedema, Yves van Leynseele, Joeri Scholtens, Courtney Vegelin, Michaela Hordijk and Winny Koster. Beyond this group, I should like to mention Boris Jansen of Natural Sciences at the UvA, with whom I conducted mind-broadening research in Africa, as well as Allister McGregor of Sheffield University in the UK, who played a defining role in the formation of my ideas on wellbeing and its importance in economics. I am grateful to my doctoral students for developing our shared ideas about the economics of wellbeing and inclusivity: Anika Altaf, Dilanthi Koralagama, Likoko Eunice, Kini Janvier, Tamara Jonkman, Olaf Erz, Raquel dos Santos, Nashia Ajaz, Rashmila Shakya and Anderson Kwasi Ahriweng. I should also like to thank my students from the Master's programme on International Development Studies for asking critical questions about 'Wellbeing Economics', and our heated discussions about power and powerlessness, freedom of choice, distribution and responsibility for minorities. They are too many to mention individually, but I should particularly like to thank Paola Gutierrez and Jennifer van Beek, who helped me with the source research. I should also like to thank Joost van Straaten, who read my work from the outset – especially for his incisive questions and requests for explanations when I descended too far into economic jargon. Finally, I should like to thank Lulu van der Meijs for her careful copyediting of this book, Jamilla van der Werff for the design of the front cover, and my publishers, Jan-Peter Wissink and Inge van der Bijl at Amsterdam University Press, who made this publication possible and encouraged me throughout.

Nicky Pouw
Amsterdam

Ten reasons why economics needs to change

1   Economics has lost touch with everyday reality.
2   Economics is based on a flawed image of human
     nature. The underlying assumptions are not
     representative of humans as social beings.
3   Economics should focus more on wellbeing and
     nature, and less on money.
4   Economics is embedded in a system of social and
     political and institutions, but these have an endoge-
     nous influence on economic processes and outcomes.
5   Economics is modelled as a closed, manageable
     system, but it is an open process with emergent
     and evolving properties.
6   Economics is defined in isolation from nature, but
     there are reciprocal relations between economics
     and nature. Human beings are dependent on nature.
7   The current economic growth model is short-
     sighted; it fails to address the long-term interests
     of social cohesion and an inclusive economy.
8   The current economic growth model prioritizes
     growth over stability; it fails to address the
     importance of social equality and sustainability.
9   Power is an underestimated factor in economics.
     Economic analysis of distribution should proble-
     matize unequal power relationships.
10   There is a need for new benchmarks in econo-
     mics. Economic progress should be measured in
     terms of the optimization of wellbeing, not the
     maximization of growth.

1 Introduction

This book is about Wellbeing Economics. This is how I view and experience economics on a daily basis, and how I hope others will (again) start to see and understand economics as an everyday practice, discipline and science. Today's economic science, with its overly narrow approach, has become too far removed from the reality of everyday life. When people think of economics, money and numbers often come to mind; we are less inclined to think about how economic choices are interwoven with social relationships, political power, psychology, nature or culture. Economics is about making choices, but economic choices are about more than money alone. Economics is also about health and wellbeing. Instead of focusing on how to maximize economic growth, in this book I argue that economics should focus on optimizing wellbeing. When weighing up economic needs and priorities, the relationships between people and with our natural surroundings play a role, as do subjective values and norms embedded in social power structures and culture. Economics should thus focus more on how to make economic choices in relation to wellbeing and nature, and less on money and cost-benefit analyses. When making economic choices, people try to protect, maintain or increase their wellbeing or that of others. There is nothing wrong with this; the majority of people want to optimize their everyday surroundings. Moreover, we live in a society where there is an increasing focus on animal wellbeing and nature. That is why I have put 'wellbeing' at the heart of this book, by which I mean both human wellbeing and the wellbeing of our surroundings, including animals. What people across the world – rich and poor, young and old, religious and atheist, women and men, prime ministers and market-traders – have in common is that they all pursue wellbeing. Their ambitions do not relate to money or property alone, however; people strive for a mix of wellbeing in a material, relational and subjective sense, and the pursuit of meaning forms part of this. It influences our daily economic choices, consciously and unconsciously. In fact, economics consists of a 'simple' aggregate of people making choices. Before making these choices, people make economic trade-offs between different options; at least, assuming they have a choice at all. In traditional economic theories, these trade-offs are made on the basis of economic cost-benefit analyses, which can be measured, modelled and even calculated numerically. In this book, however, I argue that from a wellbeing perspective this trade-off is multidimensional and consists of quantitative and qualitative values. If society values sustainability and the creation of equal opportunities, for example, and not the pursuit of economic growth alone, then we must learn to think more multi-dimensionally in economic science. Our economic models should be better at reflecting this complexity, and we should also be able to go beyond models to use a wider range of analytical methods and techniques. This could make economics a critical and relevant social science once more; one that is closer to everyday reality, and aware of the mutual dependency between humanity and nature.

In this book, I explain how and why modern economic science should be rejuvenated in order to remain a relevant scientific discipline in a changing world. In doing so, I build on the ideas of Karl Polyani (1944) and Mark Granovetter (2017) on institutionally embedded economics, George Akerlof on the role of psychology in economic behaviour (1970), Tony Lawson (1997, 2003, 2015) and the earlier work of Charles Cooley (1918) on economics as a social process (which implies that economics should thus be studied as a process), Partha Dasgupta (2007) on the relationship between humans, economics and nature, and Kate Raworth (2017) on the distributive and regenerative economy. Raworth argues that the discipline of economics is calling out for a new approach, based on sustainable social and economic limits. I agree, but I go further by proposing concrete building blocks that give a theoretical structure and content to this new vision of economics. This means that we need to go back to the fundamentals of economics and create a new framework. After all, the proposed theory and methodology should be robust. For this reason, I first consider the question: how do we define economics?

During guest lectures at the University of Amsterdam and beyond, I meet many young people, including secondary school pupils, with a great initial interest in and new ideas about economics. They tell me that they become disillusioned over time, however, and abandon further study in economics when they find out how much maths is involved and how few connections there are with social-cultural, political and environmental themes. They are taught to think that economics is just about money, and that economists mainly need to be good at arithmetic in order to develop and test economic models. That is a shame, because many of these young people have really interesting, innovative ideas about economics. Moreover, they have the ability to ask the critical, out-of-the-box questions that matter today; they are in fact perfectly placed to perceive and understand new economic phenomena, reformulate old concepts, and draw up new research questions. When it comes to being a good economist, these qualitative skills and knowledge are at least as important as quantitative knowledge and skills. In addition, deconstruction and reconstruction require knowledge of the history of economic thought. Many economic theories and models build on past work; think of the economic growth model, which has undergone multiple iterations since the Harrod-Domar model of 1939-1946, and then Robert Solow's. Those students are the people I most hope to reach and inspire with this book, followed by a broader readership of economists, lecturers, policymakers, researchers and people with a general interest in wellbeing and sustainable economics. All around the world, people are looking for new economic perspectives in order to solve current and future problems of economic distribution and sustainability. With this book, I thus hope to make a substantial contribution to the 'Rethinking Economics' debate; an initiative by an international network of students, academics and thinkers who are striving for innovation in economic thought.

Taking a wellbeing approach, I argue that the material economy is intrinsically linked to the socio-relational economy and the economics of subjective values and norms. The latter play a key role in giving meaning to our economic activities (or establishing when meaning is lacking). This means that not everything in the economy can be measured, but it can be researched. The core thesis is that 'Wellbeing Economics' is embedded in a composite of social and political institutions. In this sense, I draw on several fundamental ideas in the work of the historic political economist and social philosopher Karl Polanyi (1886-1964), and more recent work by the economic sociologist Mark Granovetter (2017). The latter argues that society and the economy are inextricably interlinked. Moreover, I make the case for more pluralism and diversity in economic science. By more pluralism, I mean that economics can be approached from a number of scientific fields, theories and principles. Pluralism is the opposite of monism – the notion that there is just one leading principle or theory in a discipline, such as one theory of economic growth or a single model for predicting growth. Pluralism means that there are multiple knowledge systems, and that a problem can be tackled using several theories and principles at the same time. This creates space for a greater diversity of social and cultural sub-systems that nurture and embed these knowledge systems and theories. A pluralistic vision of 'economics' as a science means that we should pay attention to a wider range of social-cultural and political values that play a role in shaping economic processes and outcomes, and in theory formation. As a result, an economic problem can be approached from several theoretical starting points, depending on how the question is formulated and the context; something I have become increasingly aware of in my international research on economic development and human wellbeing.[1] Pluralism also implies a greater variety of research approaches, methods and techniques. It not only opens the way to deductive (deduced from theory applying to empirical observations) and inductive (derived from empirical observations)

[1]   By 'economic development', I mean the broad structural economic changes in a society that can lead to both an improvement and a decline in human wellbeing.

methodologies, but also abductive (deduced from sufficient conditions) and retroductive (deduced from a combination of theory and empirical observation) methods. As well as econometric models based on today's monistic trend in neoclassical economics, the economist's tools should also include more heuristic exploratory approaches,[2] descriptive and narrative analyses and participatory methods. These methods require more than a good grasp of figures and mathematics alone. On the one hand, they demand an ability to reflect on causes and results in a structured and logical way, to dissect economic problems analytically, and identify potential solutions; and on the other hand, they require creative and associative thinking about new, yet-to-be-formulated relations and concepts with political, socio-cultural and natural phenomena, from a more holistic perspective.[3] At present, I see more stimulation of associative thinking skills at the margins of economics than at the core, which is dominated by linear thinking (with the exception of complexity thinking). When combined with the emphasis on quantitative research, linear thinking can lead to dissociative thinking and fall prey to one-sidedness and narrow-mindedness. Qualitative knowledge and skills, by contrast, open up the discipline of economics to external insights. This can provide a counterweight to 'inner circle thinking' and a lack of innovation in theory-formation. Pluralism does not mean that 'anything goes', however. Economic analysis should be robust at all times. By this I mean that when deviating from a certain framework or condition under which a theory or method can be applied, its basic constitution remains valid.[4] More diversity in

2   By heuristic methods, I mean non-formal research methods whereby certain criteria are used to achieve open aims in an investigative and continuously evaluative way.

3   Associative thinking is particularly important in the study of intersectionality; for example, when looking at how intersections of inequality overlap with and reinforce one another. I shall consider this in more detail in Chapter 7, 'A Focus on Inequality'.

4   In Chapter 6, 'Implications for Methodology', I look in more detail at the precise methodological implications of more pluralism in economic science for *robustness* as an underlying condition.

economics means creating more space for context and political and socio-cultural values and standards that influence decisions and processes, consciously or unconsciously. Particularly when weighing up relative values, context, politics and socio-cultural factors should play a role, and the interaction with nature should be visible. Finally, we should not underestimate the added value of creativity and originality for a good economist, both as academics and as practitioners; how else would we develop the new insights, concepts and theories, methods and indicators that are relevant for today's economy and that of the future? As Albert Einstein once said, 'creativity is intelligence having fun'. Although it is not easy to calculate the inestimable value of creativity in science, we do know that creativity is threatened when a scientific field keeps developing in accordance with monistic principles alone. To put it bluntly, one-sidedness leads to navel-gazing and the potential implosion of economic science.

Economic problems are thus always embedded in socio-cultural and political factors, the combinations of which vary in space and time. The interaction with the natural environment also influences these processes. In this book, I present the economy not as a closed, self-regulating system that is guided by an 'invisible hand', but as a concrete, human, institutionalized process that constantly interacts with this socio-cultural and political context and the natural surroundings. This epistemological starting point is further developed in Chapter 3.[5] People and their economic capacities, value judgements and options (or lack of them) play both a shaping and a leading role in the decision-making process surrounding economic problems. Human wellbeing, or human wellbeing in relation to others and the environment, is both an outcome and part of this economic process. Wellbeing should therefore play a central role in our economic thinking. As social and natural beings, people are hereby viewed expressly in relation to their living environment (see also: Dasgupta 2001). In this sense,

5   Epistemological = theory of knowledge. That is to say, how we arrive at knowledge (insights and understanding) in science, in this case economic science.

this vision also underlines the fact that nature plays a central role in the economy, because people cannot (continue to) live without nature. Whereas nature simply exists, people have to adapt to their surroundings. People can manage nature, but they can never dominate it. In the end, nature dominates humanity. A version of economics that is disconnected from nature is thus illogical, in my opinion.

Chapter 2 explains why economics needs to change, and where the deficiencies lie in the old way of economic thinking. These deficiencies are characterized by the dominance of monistic theories and atomistic methodologies. Chapter 3 explains why and how wellbeing should be put at the heart of economics, and sets out the essential differences between wellbeing economics and neoclassical thinking on welfare. In the light of this new perspective, Chapter 4 redefines economics and further develops the basic epistemological and ontological principles of 'Wellbeing Economics'. Chapter 5 introduces the Wellbeing Economics Matrix (WEM) as a logical and layered framework for economic analysis and policy planning. The methodological implications of 'Wellbeing Economics' are discussed in Chapter 6, including the combination of objective and subjective values, the use of intersections, and how to handle emergent properties in economic analysis. Based on the WEM, in Chapter 7 I propose how we should problematize and formalize economic analyses of inequality. In Chapter 8, this is followed by a similar discussion about the importance of sustainability for a healthy economy. 'Nature' is further operationalized in this chapter, and proposals are made for measuring it. By putting economic inequality and sustainability at the heart of 'Wellbeing Economics', alternative measures of economic progress become more relevant and important, and this issue forms the focus of Chapter 9. Instead of steering the economy on the basis of a limited number of economic measures, I propose that we use a 'dashboard' of indicators and measures. The book concludes with Chapter 10, where I finally discuss the potential directions and starting points for the further development of 'Wellbeing Economics'.

2   Economics (really) needs to change

Beneath the surface of neoclassical economics lies unwavering faith in the pursuit of big numbers: more is always better. More growth means more income, more supply and production, more employment, more demand, more investment, more growth, and so forth. Big numbers give people a certain sense of security; everything is 'going well' and the economy is 'healthy'. Only when a crisis hits, such as the current COVID-19 virus, do people seem to become aware of the danger that lurks in big numbers; namely, they always involve tipping points and introduce risk into other areas, such as public health or international security. By 'tipping point', I mean that a certain equilibrium is upset, such as the equilibrium in economic growth or the balance between supply and demand. However, tipping points can in themselves also upset other social, political or ecological balances, leading to disruptions in economic development in the future. At the time, the 2008 financial crisis was mainly explained as a crisis of confidence in the banking sector. The tipping point occurred when Lehman Brothers was the first bank to go bust in 2008, prompting a chain reaction of bankruptcies in the financial sector. The COVID-19 crisis of 2020 is a crisis in which the equilibrium of human health has been disrupted. It is currently thought that the crisis was caused by the consumption of the meat of certain animal species at the fish market in Wuhan, China, although this has yet to be established with certainty at the time of writing. The 2008 financial crisis and the 2020 COVID-19 crisis are two examples of global crises that clearly reveal the interconnectedness of our economies and societies. Due to our current way of life and globalization, markets, people and cultures are in constant contact with one other. We can no longer keep living in a 'throwaway society' like this, built on mass consumption and unsustainable consumption and production. Nature and human health are putting limits on this type of growth. Interlinked disruptions such as these can also occur on microeconomic or regional scales. Take the growing danger of forest fires in a country such as Portugal, for example; due to the lack of forest management and the monoculture of eucalyptus trees grown for paper production. The soil loses biomass and water, leading to serious droughts. This danger also affects other countries surrounding the Mediterranean, as a result of monocultures. Another regional example is the outbreak of Mad Cow Disease. It is no accident that large-scale bioindustry, with huge numbers of livestock packed into small spaces, is declining in many European countries with green agendas. As human beings, we should pay attention to nature as soon as big numbers develop a logic in and of themselves. Big numbers require specialized forms of production, monocultures and cost-benefit efficiency, whereas nature benefits from maximum biodiversity. In the end, it is about achieving a balance between the two: a healthy balance between large-scale and small-scale production, more and less, rich and poor, uniform and pluriform, specialism and broadening, monism and pluralism. Spreading the risk is sometimes preferable to cost-benefit efficiency; for example, to prepare the health sector for major shocks. We also need to be aware of the side-effects of big numbers, which manifest themselves inside and outside the economy and can have a boomerang effect on the entire system. Now that the COVID-19 crisis is threatening human health on a large scale and the health sector is facing major challenges, we can see disastrous side-effects emerging throughout the economy that will undermine overall growth in the long term. In order to gain a better understanding of these complex interactions, we therefore need to broaden our view of the economy. This does not mean we will be able to predict every crisis, but we may be able to spread the negative effects more effectively and minimize them where possible.

Economics in the twentieth century should therefore focus more on people, nature, and the wellbeing and preservation of both, and less on money. Although economic growth is important to keep the economy going, it can never be an end-goal in itself. This argument has been made since the 1970s by Amartya Sen, the Indian economist and philosopher and winner of the 1998 Nobel Prize in Economics. In his work, Sen argues that we should focus more on human values and culture in economics, and less on monism and methodological individualism. This is because the economy depends on interpersonal relationships, as well as interactions between humans and nature. These relationships are shaped by the spirit of the age, location and culture. Humans will also be dependent on our environmental surroundings for as long as we live on this Earth, and make use of its energy and natural space. This dependence is overlooked in neoclassical economics, however, due to the latter's emphasis on monistic theoretical abstractions of unlimited rationality,[6] unlimited egoism, boundless willpower and stable preferences. Taken together, these assumptions are also the key reasons for the critique of 'methodological individualism', which is known as a core fallacy in neoclassical economics. What is meant by this? It is a complex argument that requires further explanation.[7] On the one hand, Amartya Sen criticizes the theoretical content and basic epistemological principles of economics, and, on the other hand, the methodology that results from this (see further Chapter 3).[8]

Let us first address the theoretical substantive argument. Although the assumptions of unlimited egoism and rationality, or rather individual interest and cost-benefit efficiency, are important mechanisms for economic decision-making and allocation, they are certainly not the only motivations driving people's economic choices. Even when buying shares, corporate social responsibility or the sustainability of the company in

---

6   The philosophical view that just one thing – one theory, in this case – is valid.
7   The complete explanation for this assumption of 'methodological individu-alism' is extended over parts of Chapters 2 & 3.
8   By methodology, I mean the strategy used to conduct the research, consisting of one or several types of research methods for gathering and analysing data.

question can be important considerations, in addition to psychology and emotion. This is reflected in current trends towards social and green entrepreneurship and sustainable investment, and the emergence of sustainable and ethical banks, such as Triodos bank in the Netherlands. Triodos has grown its business by supporting environmentally-friendly, social and cultural enterprises. Human and institutional economic decisions relating to production, consumption and distribution are partly determined by a whole range of other motivations, such as force of habit, misgivings, idealism, morality, competitive behaviour, copycat behaviour ('keeping up with the Joneses'), helpfulness, charity, or extortion and exploitation. Economic decisions can be taken on the basis of an awareness of sustainability or time and concern for future generations. Socio-cultural and political preferences therefore shape economic choices, meaning that they are not always 'rational' from a cost-benefit perspective, or exclusively serve short-term gain or self-interest.

The assumption of 'unlimited willpower' is likewise criticized by behavioural economics and other heterodox economists, because economic choices are also influenced by the psychology of human behaviour as well as by political factors and power – or the lack of these (for example, acting out of powerlessness). At the same time, people have limited willpower to solve economic problems rationally. Psychological factors such as pessimism or resignation, or a lack of knowledge and skill, also play a role in this, as does the interweaving of human motivations and behaviour with political factors and rules. Immigrants have little or no access to another country's formal labour market, for example, until they have acquired a residence permit. At the present time, the entanglement of economic and political interests is playing a major role in the discussion surrounding the law on firearms in the United States. Due to its incessant government lobbying, the National Rifle Association, a pressure group that campaigns for the right of American citizens to possess firearms, is one of the country's most powerful and politically influential organizations, with strong links to the American firearms industry. The freedom to possess a firearm is also strongly defended by many American citizens. In times of crisis, such as the COVID-19 crisis of 2020, we unfortunately see many citizens taking up weapons driven by fear of social unrest, rather than investing in solidarity. Political power and inequality thus play a role when we make economic choices; at least, when people have the freedom to choose something. Not everyone has a free choice or can choose between good options. For example, feminist economists have been arguing for decades that economic decision-making is influenced by gender inequalities and conventions. We need only consider the pay gap between women and men doing the same jobs, or the legislative history of female participation in the job market, to understand what this means. Political power and inequality put real limits on 'willpower' and the extent to which freedom of choice actually exists at all.

Furthermore, since 1979 behavioural economists such as Daniel Kahneman and Amos Tversky have been arguing, based on prospect theory, that economic choice behaviour is context-specific and that people consequently attach more importance to relative value than to absolute value. In other words, when choosing between two possible alternatives, a and b, the estimated risk of loss is not absolute, but will partly depend on the previous situation (and is thus relative). On average, people consider the risk of loss to outweigh the promise of gain, and certainties to outweigh opportunities. The certainty effect plays an important role when people make economic choices. In this way, Kahneman and Tversky show that future expectations and psychology play a role in economics. They show that at the point of making a choice, the overlap between the disciplines of psychology and economics is so great that it is sometimes difficult to distinguish between the two at all; both at the micro-level of individuals and households and at the institutional and macro-level, where aggregated factors such as 'consumer confidence' can influence whole sectors and economic growth figures and stability.

Finally, critics have long contested the assumption of stable preferences in neoclassical economics. Despite this, the assumption of stable preferences within a data set is still frequently used in economic models. This assumption allows economists to model the behaviour of a calculating and sovereign (self-determining) individual as consistent. That is to say, the preferences of this individual in relation to a set of possible choices remain the same in the short term, which facilitates economic modelling and prediction over time. However, the assumption of stable preferences is undermined by factors such as limited rationality,[9] the way in which options are presented, and the role of context; and because unstable preferences are difficult to model, this often only comes up in the reflective comments on the limitations of the research.

Economists who have recently worked on complexity theory have made some progress in modelling these factors, meaning that certain assumptions can already be included in the analysis. They refer to 'tipping points' in economic trends, for example, and 'feedback mechanisms' from context to model, demonstrating their acceptance of unstable preferences. These theoretical assumptions have important methodological consequences, and I shall discuss these implications further in Chapter 6.

For now, it suffices to say that in light of the critique of methodological individualism, 'preferences' has become a convoluted concept.[10] Continuing to use it in a new vision of 'Wellness Economics' would thus lead to confusion and misconceptions. In the following chapters, I therefore prefer to use the terms 'needs' and 'priorities'. Human needs, such as for food or drinking

9   The psychologist and sociologist Herbert Simon formulated a number of axioms that characterize his decision-making theory and the idea of limited (or bounded) rationality, including limited knowledge of alternatives, limited capacity to compare all alternatives rationally, sub-optimal choices because the first option is prioritized to satisfy a need, the impact of routine, and the relative dominance of the simultaneous (rather than the sequential) comparative mode (Simon 1957).
10   In science, we refer to a 'convoluted concept' when a concept has acquired so many meanings (over time) that its meaning becomes ambiguous and not recognizable as such.

water, security and self-actualization, are defined as forms of deprivation of which we are aware, prompting a desire for what is lacking. Priorities are expressions of relative preferences about the various choice dimensions of wellbeing, which can change over time and aggregation level. Needs and priorities can converge, but they can also differ. After all, someone who is hungry may prioritize political freedom over food, despite the deprivation they are suffering. Priorities can also differ between an individual and other people or their environment. As an individual, someone might see striving for a higher income as a priority, but might not consider this a priority for the household or community in which they live. Priorities can also change over time and are context-dependent. This is addressed in more depth in Chapter 3, in relation to the multi-dimensional concept of wellbeing.

In conclusion, I want to emphasize that political power, culture, psychology, emergent and evolving phenomena and the relationship between humans and nature make economics a complex science; and this is hardly surprising, as human beings are complex creatures. The problem is that in recent decades, many economic theories have lost sight of human relations and nature, and thereby of relational and subjective human wellbeing. Instead, economists have become increasingly adept at developing econometric models based on theories that have little to do with what it means to be human. Businesses, governments and institutions are viewed as though humans did not form a crucial part of them, but only the production factors derived from humans, such as labour, technology and capital. In order to become more and more advanced, these models are increasingly concerned with measurable factors (quantity and monetary values), and less and less with humans as social beings. As a science and as field of knowledge, economics has become 'inhuman', as it were. The contorted pursuit of (apparent)[11] objectivity and

11   The notion that numbers and monetary indicators only 'appear' to be objective and are never completely objective is a methodological critique that I shall address further in Chapter 6.

precision can easily come at the expense of a realistic portrayal of human nature as a guiding perspective in economics. 'Homo economicus' represents a flawed self-image of what it means to be human, one that has little to do with our everyday economic identity and actions. Who would recognize themselves in the calculating 'loner' who is isolated from everything and everyone? Even Robinson Crusoe needed Man Friday to keep him company, and he ultimately survived thanks to this company and to nature.

The pursuit of objectivity and exact science has led to an emphasis in economic research on secondary criteria such as measurability, verifiability and predictability, with a grounding in existing knowledge about the past. Primary wellbeing criteria, such as quality of life, freedom, solidarity and connection, and sustainability have thereby become less important. In the process, economic science has lost its direct relevance to the economic problems of today and tomorrow; that is, to issues such as globalization, distribution and sustainability. This realization again became painfully clear during the global financial crisis of 2007-8. And that is why, with this book, I want to put the relations between humanity and nature, and thereby the constant pursuit of human wellbeing, at the heart of economic science. It is why we need to view people in relation to their surroundings, and not as atomistic individuals.[12] It is a way to ground economics – with all its facets and functions – more effectively, and to penetrate the fast-changing economic processes, categories and structures, global relations, new phenomena and outcomes around us; and in this way, economics will also regain relevance. Rather than people, we have made money, as a measure of individual welfare, the most important subject in economics. As Amartya Sen argued (1980), however, money can never be an end-goal in itself; it is only

12 In political philosophy, 'atomism' is the notion that society consists merely of separate individuals. Those who endorse this vision also argue that although there are connections between individuals, these connections are based entirely on free choice. This philosophy thus leaves no room for socio-cultural institutions, for example, or the power relations that are characteristic of interpersonal relations.

a means of exchange (and perhaps an impermanent one at that). Also, like money, growth cannot be an end in itself. The current process of globalization has given rise to challenges of sustainability and increasing inequality. Money and growth may be easy to calculate, but this is no reason to see econometric models as the sole set of instruments available to the economist. This has a range of methodological implications, which I discuss further in Chapter 6. Economics therefore needs to change; economists need to shift their focus away from money, and back towards people, nature, and the greater common good of our everyday pursuit of wellbeing.

3   A focus on wellbeing

Economics should thus be more concerned with wellbeing, and less concerned with money. But what do we actually mean by 'wellbeing'? It is a term that is frequently used in different countries and cultures. In some Latin American countries, for example, the terms *buen vivir* ('live well') and *sumak kawsai* ('complete life') are used; in Africa, we come across *ubuntu* ('attachment to life and human relations') and *hunhu* ('being human as part of a community'); and in Asia, Buddhism uses term *sukha* ('reducing suffering') and Hinduism uses *dharma* ('the morality of human action') to express something similar to 'wellbeing' (see also Table 1). Wellbeing is *not* synonymous with individual happiness. Happiness and wellbeing are linked, but wellbeing never precludes unhappiness or suffering. It would be impossible to pursue a political policy that focused on making everyone happy, because individuals themselves play the greatest role in this, but policy *can* focus on promoting wellbeing. In his research on wellbeing and international development,[13] Allister McGregor defines wellbeing as: *'a state of being with others, where human needs are met, where one can act meaningfully to pursue one's goals, and where one enjoys a satisfactory quality of life'* (source: McGregor 2007). Just like other international terms, this definition of wellbeing stems from the assumption that human beings are *social beings*;[14] after all, every person has relationships with other people and with the natural environment. These relationships are not always based on free choice, but are partly determined by birth and location. Moreover, every person relates to a particular time; we

13   The concept of 'wellbeing' has global relevance, one that is independent of wealth or poverty in any sense.

14   In this book, I focus on human wellbeing. I also discuss the wellbeing of nature, which includes animal wellbeing. This is why I do not mention animal wellbeing separately each time, although it is indeed of great intrinsic and extrinsic importance to a sustainable economy.

all have a past, present and future. The difference between the above-mentioned synonyms for 'wellbeing' in various countries and cultures is one of emphasis. Whereas the African *ubuntu* emphasizes community ('we-ness'), the Asian *dharma* puts greater emphasis on the moral behaviour of the individual; how can we do good for others? Other concepts of wellbeing emphasize the relationship between humans and nature (e.g., in Buddhism), whereby the idea of the 'self' is a consequence of the separation between humans and nature. These concepts of wellbeing can be traced back historically to specific cultures and ways of living, which explains the differences in emphasis. But what all of these concepts share is that wellbeing is a comprehensive concept, in which the reciprocal interconnections between and dependencies of people (between people themselves, between people and nature, and between people and their mental wellbeing and spirituality) play a central role. In addition, wellbeing always has a subjective element; how it is experienced. In short, *wellbeing thinking focuses on a theory of humans as social beings, as part of nature and as meaning-givers.* The fact that people also have individualistic and rational qualities does not mean that they can be reduced in a one-dimensional fashion to rational, calculating individuals. This would not provide a representative picture of humanity.

Once we become aware of the significance of human wellbeing, it is easier to grasp the fact that people make economic decisions based on more than self-interest alone; people also think and act, consciously or unconsciously, on the basis of their relationships with the other people around them, as well as their surroundings and personal convictions. Moreover, people make economic decisions based a broader notion of time than the 'here and now'. People think ahead to the future, back to the past and in the present, and make economic decisions based on these complex temporal considerations in an entirely individual way. Some decisions are not theirs to make; in some cases, they lack freedom of choice. The concept of 'wellbeing' covers the material, relational and subjective aspects of humanity. In addition, I want

Table 1   Overview of different wellbeing concepts

Concept	Definition	Philosophy	Core values
Happiness	Individual satis-faction; subjective wellbeing	Individualism; utilitarianism; positivism	Emphasis on individual utility; individual freedom and responsibility
Wellbeing	Doing good and living well in relation to others and surroundings; material, relational and subjective wellbeing	Humanism	Reason, ethics of human values and justice
Buen vivir, Sumak kawsai (Latin America)	Living well together; solidarity with others	Humanism; anti-utilitarianism; solidarity	Unity
Ubuntu, Hunhu (Africa)	Oneness; dedica-tion and relations between people and after death	Humanism	Group comes be-fore the individual; dignity of ancestors; consensus
Dharma (Asia – Hinduism and Buddhism)	Morality; norms and rules of personal and social behaviour	Hedonism; spiritualism	Human dignity within emotional (pleasure), political-economic, moral and metaphysical dimensions
Sukha (Asia – Buddhism)	Happiness, pleasure, congenia-lity, blessing	Spiritualism; anti-materialism	Physical and mental happiness

Source: the author, assisted by Paola Gutierrez

to emphasize that 'wellbeing' is a dynamic concept; wellbeing is simultaneously an outcome and a process of the human pursuit of self-preservation, stability and/or improvement. This can relate to someone's material condition, but also to their health, or a feeling of security and interconnectedness with humanity and nature. Finally, it will have become clear that wellbeing has both objective and subjective aspects. For example, every person has an objective need for food and drink, a sense of security and freedom, but the extent and form of these needs is subjective and context-dependent. As a process and as an outcome, wellbeing is therefore partly subjective. After all, not everyone pursues the same life-goals, acts on the basis of the same values and norms, or the same religion or philosophy of life. Material wealth does not imply shared humanity, a sustainable lifestyle, happiness or satisfaction, but some people do use their material wealth to help others or protect nature.

Wellbeing versus welfare

In this book, the term 'wellbeing' is used to mean something different from, and even more than, welfare. It is important to clarify this difference, because the two concepts are used interchangeably in the literature. Welfare, to use the term as it has been defined in the history of economic science, refers to the degree to which human needs can be met in the event of scarcity. Scarcity is key to this definition; it means that resources are depleted with use. In neoclassical economics, the emphasis has long been on studying allocation problems under conditions of scarcity. Now that the economic value of natural resources and space is increasingly being recognized as an important source of ecosystem services, the emphasis of economic analysis has shifted from absolute to relative scarcity. Some ecosystem services, such as solar and wind energy, are scarcer in a relative sense, because not everyone has access to the associated technology, while the quantity of solar and wind energy need not be scarce/less scarce in an absolute sense. For this reason, more recent definitions of economic allocation problems are increasingly dropping the notion of 'scarcity'.

Welfare is usually measured by economists at the national level using Gross National Product (GNP); the total added value of all goods and services produced in a particular country within a certain period, or as an aggregation of all incomes. At an individual level, welfare is usually measured with a monetary indicator of consumption (expenditure) or income per head of the population. In neoclassical economic theory, welfare is linked to the fundamental idea that every individual acts rationally when making economic decisions. This means that economic decisions are made on the basis of a cost-benefit efficiency trade-off expressed in monetary terms. It is argued that if every individual acts efficiently and in accordance with self-interest, and thus rationally, that this will lead, by means of an 'invisible hand' as it were, to the maximization of everyone's welfare. There has been much criticism of rationality theory within economics, something we will consider in more depth in Chapter 3.

For now, let us focus on the concept of welfare. We have arrived at the next part of the explanation of methodological individualism that we began in Chapter 2; the part of the explanation that criticizes the economic methodology that accompanies ideas about welfare. The basic principle of welfare thinking in neoclassical economics is that people derive individual utility from welfare. Utility is the enjoyment or satisfaction that people derive from a package of goods or services – which can partly be purchased with income, but also as public goods and services (education, for example, or public space). The level of utility achieved is described as 'welfare'; the degree to which needs can be met with scarce resources. Welfare theory is based on the principle that individual utility can be aggregated into collective utility. Collective utility is thus synonymous with 'social welfare', such as the social welfare of a community, group of people, city or country. This only makes sense if we assume that utility is continuous; that is to say, that utility is one-dimensional and can be aggregated using an unambiguous measure (such as income or spending, expressed in monetary terms). The pursuit of maximal individual welfare then becomes synonymous with the maximization of social welfare, because the latter is simply the numerical consequence of the former. After all, $1+1$ is always more than 1, and $1+1+1+ \dots n$ is thus always more than $1+1+1+ \dots$ n-1. The question, however, is whether the original theorists of welfare actually had such a narrow concept of welfare in mind.

If we re-read Adam Smith's *Theory of Moral Sentiments* (1759), for example, it is clear that Smith saw nature as the greatest source of welfare. Moreover, the relations between man and nature are based on more than utility alone; nature is also a source of spiritual wellbeing, and natural space is needed for social space. The neoclassical reduction of 'welfare' to individual utility that is only calculated on a one-dimensional scale was evidently necessary in order to formulate an economic model and delineate economic trade-offs 'objectively', and to make them measurable and mutually comparable. Within an economic model, it is then quite straightforward to make calculations with this measurable utility variable. Economic comparisons can be calculated more objectively when they consist of quantifiable and unambiguous relations. Objective comparisons can be made in both a vertical direction, from the lowest (individual welfare) to the highest scale level (global welfare), and in a horizontal direction (between economic agents), albeit with the necessary adjustments for context-specific differences in price and purchasing power. Comparisons can even be made relatively simply over time, subject to methodological consistency and with the usual adjustments for price differences and inflation. In this book, however, I argue that economic models need not be constructed using measurable variables alone; a more pluralistic methodology will be discussed in more detail in Chapter 6. Finally, here it is important to mention the 'broad concept of welfare' championed by the Dutch economist Arnold Heertje (2006). To counter the narrow concept of welfare, the term 'broad welfare' has been adopted in the Dutch context (by arithmeticians at Statistics Netherlands, among others).[15] 'Broad welfare' is

15   Since 2015, Statistics Netherlands' working group on 'Broad Welfare' has been working to define and measure social and sustainability indicators that are not measured by GNP. For more information, see the memo 'CBS Activiteiten op het gebied van brede welvaart en duurzaamheid [Activities of Statistics Netherlands in the field of broad welfare and sustainability]', 10 September 2015, and follow-up publications such as the 'Monitor Brede Welvaart en de SDGs 2019 [Monitor Broad Welfare and the SDGs 2019]'.

likewise concerned with social progress and distribution, as well as quality of life. As such, it comes close to Allister McGregor's concept of wellbeing. But there is also a difference: whereas the social and subjective dimensions of wellbeing are used alongside one another in the broad concept of welfare, McGregor conceives of them as being inherently intertwined.

The three dimensions of wellbeing

Wellbeing thus covers more than welfare, and it has both objective and subjective elements. Someone might be doing well in terms of their general health and employment, for example, but if they feel structurally insecure or are not free to express their opinions or practise their religion, their overall sense of wellbeing may nevertheless be poor. Implicit in this alternative line of reasoning is a broader concept of 'welfare'; one in which more factors than monetary values alone (or other one-dimensional material values) count in the translation from individual to collective utility derived from welfare. To this end, Allister McGregor and I have proposed, in abstract terms, a multidimensional concept of 'wellbeing' (source: 'Towards an Economics of Wellbeing' in the *Cambridge Journal of Economics,* 2016).[16] After all, wellbeing refers to 'a state of being in relation to others', and it is this relationship that can develop either positively or negatively, and can thus transform a relationship on a different scale level and over time. From now on, therefore, I prefer to refer to 'wellbeing' as a state that people pursue in their daily economic actions, so as to avoid any confusion with the oft-used concept of 'welfare'. Exactly what this means for the definition of 'economics' will be addressed in more detail in Chapter 4, 'What is Economics?'.

16   Driven by a similar motivation, Costanza and colleagues also argue for a central focus on wellbeing in economics in their article 'Towards a Sustainable Wellbeing Economy' (2018).

First, however, I want to take a more detailed look at the alternative concept of 'wellbeing', and why this concept should replace the concept of welfare in both its narrow and broad versions. The economy is not a self-regulating system. Ultimately, it is people themselves, and not some kind of 'invisible hand', who steer economic processes and outcomes with the aim of protecting, maintaining and/or improving human wellbeing. As explained above, human wellbeing is an abstract and comprehensive concept, which needs clearer definition if we wish to apply it further in economic science. In his theory of wellbeing, Allister McGregor makes an analytical distinction (source: McGregor, 2007) between three dimensions:

(i)   material wellbeing; the objective, observable outcomes that people are able to achieve, such as food, accommodation, possessions, income, work, physical and built environment;

(ii)   relational wellbeing; the resources that people have and their relations with others and their natural surroundings that allow them to fulfil their needs and aims, such as civil rights, security, self-determination and power, partnership, solidarity, altruism, networking, sustainability and freedom;

(iii) subjective wellbeing; the meanings and values that people ascribe to the needs and aims that they can achieve and the processes that they undertake for this purpose, such as (dis)satisfaction, frustration, internal conflict, (in)security, happiness, aspiration and mental wellbeing.

These three dimensions of wellbeing are interwoven with one another and over time, and all aspects of material and relational wellbeing can be linked to a subjective experience or perception of wellbeing. The distinction is thus purely analytical, and often difficult to make in practice. In this sense, it differs from the broad concept of welfare, which considers the different elements in isolation. For example, 'human health' can be measured partly objectively (e.g., heart rate, body mass index, blood pressure), as well as being a relational and subjective personal experience

('I feel perfectly healthy compared to other people' or 'I feel lousy' are statements that can be made by individuals who are ostensibly equally healthy), and an external quality that is partly cultural and shaped by the spirit of the age (being heavier is an indication of personal wellbeing in many cultures). Nevertheless, I take these three dimensions of wellbeing as a key starting point for developing this new vision of economics. People's economic behaviour is characterized by a constant striving to protect, maintain and/or improve their wellbeing, as individuals, groups, or societies. The extent to which they are able to do this is dependent on the resources, capacities and freedoms that are available. Efforts and goals to achieve wellbeing can be focused on one or more dimensions of wellbeing, and on different scale levels. For example, one might pursue spiritual wellbeing and want to live in relative social seclusion as an individual, but pursue a certain degree of cohesion and basic security as a family, and pursue a certain level of material wellbeing as a society. At the same time, a very wealthy individual might pursue optimal material wellbeing for themselves and their family by placing family members in prominent social positions, for example, but might never succeed in achieving a sense of satisfaction or happiness.

We cannot simply assume that wellbeing is a free choice, however; after all, not every person has the power and resources to make choices at all, let alone in a self-assured and informed way. People who live in deep material and social poverty and are politically marginalized, such as outcasts in Indian society, are often able to do little more than protect their precarious existence for good or ill, whilst sacrificing basic forms of self-esteem, spiritual wellbeing and human happiness. The constant pursuit of optimal wellbeing as the greatest common denominator in human economic behaviour is visualized in Figure 1. Note that this figure shows wellbeing as both an outcome and as a process. Wellbeing is also dynamic – it changes over time – and economic choices are made with an awareness of the past, present and future. This means that there are historical connections between

Figure 1   The constant pursuit of optimal wellbeing

Material wellbeing
Relational wellbeing
Subjective wellbeing

Improvement

Wellbeing

Source: taken from Pouw and McGregor 2014

the economic choices that people make, something that is rarely captured in economic models. In many economic models, economic choices (and outcomes) are modelled as idiosyncratic (self-standing) events. By contrast, Figure 1 shows that present and future wellbeing are partly dependent on wellbeing in the past, and *vice versa*.

For decades, the above-mentioned assumption of 'methodological individualism' in traditional economics has been contested by heterodox economists,[17] as well as by various groups outside the discipline of economics. Critics argue that every aggregation

17   'Heterodox economics' is an umbrella term for a varying list of alternative (non-mainstream) trends in economic science that do not necessarily have more in common than criticism of the 'mainstream'. At present, the field of heterodox economics (more or less) includes the following: Marxist economics, feminist economics, political economics, anthropological economics, behavioural economics, and so forth.

of individual utility into collective utility, for example from the individual to the household, or from the household to the national population, is coupled with an exchange of other values that influence and transform the collective utility that is eventually achieved. In other words, a *qualitative* transformation of the utility relations between these people (or households) takes place, whereby the collective utility derived from social welfare is greater or smaller than the aggregation of the separate parts. This transformation takes place through effects of complementarity, exchange (substitution), strengthening and weakening, feedback and anticipation. In short, as a consequence of this qualitative transformation, the aggregation of the utility derived from the individual welfare of individual 1 (NWV_1) and individual 2 (NWV_2) can be *more or less than* (NWV_1+NWV_2), and is not *sine qua non* an aggregation that can be used to measure collective utility on a scale. Building on this, it is then no longer logical to assume that social welfare is maximized when individual utility functions are maximized, nor is it logical to presume that if we maximize economic growth, humanity and the planet will be better off.

From now on, I shall therefore refer to the 'optimization of wellbeing', rather than the maximization of individual welfare. As wellbeing is multidimensional and consists of objective and subjective values, I shall represent the aggregation of individual wellbeing functions as a *cross-section* of two sets, instead of as an aggregation of individual utility functions. The cross-section of two sets of wellbeing functions is represented mathematically as: $NWV_1 \cap NWV_2$. The outcome of such an aggregation can thus be *more or less or equal to* the sum of individual wellbeing functions; in other words:

- $NWV_1 \cap NWV_2 < NWV_1 + NWV_2$: collective wellbeing is smaller than the aggregation of individual wellbeing.
- $NWV_1 \cap NWV_2 > NWV_1 + NWV_2$: collective wellbeing is larger than the aggregation of individual wellbeing.
- $NWV_1 \cap NWV_2 = NWV_1 + NWV_2$: collective wellbeing is equal to the aggregation of individual wellbeing.

Economic choices from a wellbeing perspective

When making economic choices (when people have the freedom and opportunity to do so), and trying to solve economic problems (when people have the willpower and knowledge to do so), a number of trade-offs are made, sequentially or simultaneously. After all, one economic decision (and its result) has consequences for another economic decision (and its result), in the same or one/several dimensions of human wellbeing. But these consequences are not limited to the individual. The economic decision made by a person, group or organization can have an effect on the wellbeing of another person, group or organization. These consequences are again multidimensional and lie in the present, past and future. This can perhaps be seen most clearly in the way in which our generation is using ecosystem services. What happens today, in terms of environmental pollution and extraction, has direct implications for the wellbeing of societies in the near future. The study of economics is concerned, among other things, with recognizing patterns in the way that people make economic choices. By now it should be clear that from a wellbeing perspective, these choices are not one-dimensional, nor do they relate to one another consistently over time. Interim changes can take place, resulting in people deviating from a previously chosen path (or pattern). Finally, but not insignificantly, socio-cultural and political power relations affect economic relations, and the relative freedom in which making any kind of choice is possible for any person, regardless of their origin, nationality, ethnicity, sex, skin colour or beliefs etc. Political power is rarely unrelated to economic influence, and *vice versa*; although the degree of reciprocity is dependent on the political order and society. However it may be, economics is not free from political power relations, and this applies to the microlevel of the household, the business world, communities and social groups, right up to the macrolevel of sectors, national and regional economics, and the international level of organizations, markets and agencies.

What economists call 'preferences' are choice preferences which are captured in neoclassical economic models as one-dimensional constants. In reality however, people's preferences can change over time. For this reason, here I prefer to introduce the alternative concept of 'priorities' to clarify this distinction with preferences (see also Chapter 3), as well as continuing to refer to needs. Priorities are economic preferences that are multidimensional and can change over time, both in a positive and a negative sense. People can prioritize one or more dimensions of wellbeing in their economic behaviour. Although a priority can remain the same for a long period of time, it is temporary by nature. This temporariness is partly determined by changes in one or more dimensions of wellbeing, but it can also come about as a consequence of an external 'shock'. An exchange or trade-off takes place between the three dimensions of wellbeing. This trade-off is complex, meaning that not only are the dimensions interrelated, but there are also feedback mechanisms, and all of this happens at different scale levels – for example, feedback between an individual and collective feeling of security.

The three dimensions of wellbeing and the relations between them are shown in the Venn diagrams in Figure 2. A Venn diagram is a useful first step in reflecting logically on an abstract concept such as wellbeing, and how the different dimensions of wellbeing can in theory relate to one another in all possible ways. There are several intersections (overlaps) between the three dimensions of wellbeing: between material and subjective wellbeing ($M \cap S$), between material and relational wellbeing ($M \cap R$), between relational and subjective wellbeing ($R \cap S$), and between all three ($M \cap R \cap S$) simultaneously. These intersections show where different dimensions of wellbeing in people's choice behaviour coincide, but without presupposing that this:

(+) *is a positive relationship, involving complementarity or optimization:*

$M \cap S > M + S$

$R \cap S > R + S$

$M \cap R > M + R$

$M \cap S \cap R > M + S + R$

(-) *is a negative relationship, involving undermining or sub-optimization:*

$M \cap S < M + S$

$R \cap S < R + S$

$M \cap R < M + R$

$M \cap S \cap R < M + S + R$

(+/-) *is a neutral relationship, which can sometimes involve substitution:*

$M \cap S = M + S$

$R \cap S = R + S$

$M \cap R = M + R$

$M \cap S \cap R = M + S + R$

The symbol for the intersection ($\cap$) can differ significantly for each individual, group, organization or society, and is partly dependent on personal and structural factors. In the case of a positive interaction, the relationship will be complementary; that is to say that the two aspects of wellbeing supplement and reinforce one other (like a 'multiplier'). For example, a wealthy person with many relatives ($M+S$) can derive added value ($M \cap S$) from sharing their wealth with their large family ($M \cap S > M + S$), because they consider this to be valuable and it gives them pleasure. By contrast, a wealthy person with many relatives ($M+S$) may experience less wellbeing ($M \cap S < M + S$) because they are expected to share everything with their family. The eventual outcome depends, among other things, on the initial position, life phase and experience of happiness. Someone who has always been relatively poor, and is now relatively rich, may experience their relatives' expectations as a form of pressure. But the outcome also depends on personal characteristics; some people are stingy by nature, others are not. Finally, many people take pleasure in sharing their wealth with others later in life. If it makes little difference to someone whether they share their wealth with their relatives, we describe this as a neutral relationship between two aspects of wellbeing ($M \cap S = M + S$). This notation for the three dimensions of wellbeing is also used later in Chapter 5, when explaining the Wellbeing Economics Matrix (Table 2). The intersection sign is key in the aggregation procedure, because it distinguishes between the observations (points) that are measured within the intersection, and the observations (points) outside the intersection areas.

In a Venn diagram, it is difficult to show that the intersections between the three dimensions of wellbeing can influence each other on different scale levels. In other words, the Venn diagram is layered. We will elaborate further on this point when we start to formulate these economic relations using mathematical functions; for now, it is suffice to say that the Venn diagram (Figure 2) should actually be seen as three-dimensional, with the depth measure showing the different aggregation levels (see further Chapter 5).

Thus, aside from this trade-off between the three dimensions of wellbeing, there is also exchange between individual and collective wellbeing, whereby 'collective' can refer to different aggregation levels: from the household to a social group, community or neighbourhood, to a village or town, to a region, province, country or countries. People weigh up their self-interest (often unconsciously) against the collective interest; for example, out of an obligatory moral or cultural tendency to act socially and give up part of their paid working time to do volunteer work. Finally, there is a trade-off between wellbeing in the present, past and future. Consider how many parents save in order to invest in education for their offspring, so that their children – and perhaps they, too – can enjoy a better future. And does a society prioritize economic growth in the short term, regardless of the wellbeing costs in terms of social equality or sustainability?

Figure 2   The intersections between the three dimensions of wellbeing

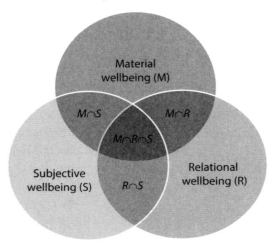

Source: Pouw and McGregor 2014

How do these priorities change over time? Something that is a relative priority at one moment may take second place the next, because a previous priority has been fulfilled. When a country manages to limit its carbon emissions to a certain maximum level, for example, its investment priorities may shift from clean energy to education. Thus, at multiple scale levels in the economy (described by economists as 'aggregation' levels), trade-offs are constantly being made between and within different dimensions of wellbeing. The existence of such multidimensional trade-offs at multiple economic scale levels may make the analysis of economic behaviour much more complex than for the individualistic and one-dimensional concept of welfare, but they do not make it less relevant. On the contrary, lying at the heart of the wellbeing perspective is a more plausible image of humanity (man as a social being) than in the welfare perspective (man as a purely rational, calculating individual). Let us take a moment to reflect on which portrayal of humanity is more realistic. *Humans are mutually dependent on each other and on the natural environment in order to be able to survive as a species.* When we accept this mutual dependence as a basic principle, it is actually extremely sensible to see social wellbeing and sustainability as being at least as worthy a pursuit as individual wellbeing or economic growth.[18] If we take good care of others and nature, we indirectly take good care of ourselves. Elinor Ostrom (1933-2012)[19] argued that societies would soon cease to exist if they consisted exclusively of self-maximizing, atomistic individuals. Compared to the welfare perspective, I believe the wellbeing perspective to be a much more realistic portrayal of everyday life and people's conduct as economic agents, because people are defined as *social beings,* rather than exclusively as rationalizing individualists. We cannot (continue to) exist without one another. The wellbeing perspective thus brings economic science closer to everyday reality, as well as to our experience and ability to imagine new economic phenomena and ideas. This imaginative power is important for thinking outside the old frameworks and coming up with new theories. By regaining relevance to today's global economic problems, wellbeing thinking has the potential to greatly enrich economic science. By putting a broad concept such as wellbeing, rather than the narrow notion of welfare, at the heart of economics, we (again) create channels to other sciences and disciplines, as well as the latitude, openness and creativity that are sorely needed for more pluralistic thinking. However, we cannot speak of a totally 'new vision of economics' if we simply exchange one key concept ('wellbeing') for another ('welfare'). If we were subsequently to focus only on how to measure wellbeing, we would fail in our aim of fundamentally rejuvenating economic

18   I could have used the word 'rational' again here, but avoided doing so, because this might create confusion with the use of the rationality principle in neoclassical economics, which was criticized above.

19   Elinor Ostrom was the first woman to win the Nobel Prize in Economics – albeit as a non-economist, as she was a political scientist. She was awarded the prize jointly with Oliver E. Williamson in 2009 for her 'analysis of economic governance, especially the commons' (1999). In this, she explains how institutions develop for purposes of collective action and economic governance.

science. More building blocks and insights – indeed, a whole new foundation – are needed in order to achieve real theoretical innovation in economic science. This will entail a series of related ontological, epistemological, theoretical and methodological revisions of economic science, focused on 'human wellbeing'. It goes without saying that the alternative proposals at each of these knowledge levels should be logically linked. Although this book does not claim to be comprehensive in this respect, several fundamental revisions will be addressed in the discussion of economic concepts and theory in Chapter 4, and the analytical framework and methodology in Chapters 5 and 6. With this book, I am thus inviting others to join me in reflecting on the further development of this new vision of economics based on wellbeing thinking. Not only will this require more conceptual and theoretical innovation, but also – and particularly – methodological innovation. This book does not claim to have found all of the answers; the aim is to make a fundamental start on the new 'Wellbeing Economics' in order to inspire and stimulate other economists and non-economists, students and interested parties.

4   What is economics?

In Chapter 2, I argued that the economics presented in today's textbooks has become almost 'inhuman'; in any case, it has lost its sense of common humanity. It also lacks a focus on the interactions between humans and nature. I therefore proposed in Chapter 3 that wellbeing should be put at the heart of economics. It is difficult to trace the human factor in economic models, however; human preferences are reduced to a number of vectors, whilst the aggregation of these is extrapolated to the greatest common good. This contains a great contradiction, leading to misconceptions in economics. Although many economic studies claim to be about 'human behaviour', the real human perspective is lost. This is partly understandable; in the process of abstracting from reality to an economic law or model, the research subject loses its multidimensionality. However, when this is done using a skewed image of humanity (the rational, calculating individual), the human perspective is lost altogether and humans and being-human become unrecognizable in the economic analysis. After all, the focus has shifted to the methodology of reduction to monetary units. Everything of value is measured on a one-dimensional scale. People are not one-dimensional, though; people make choices based on multiple interests and value judgements, some of which conflict. This makes economic decision-making complex and difficult to predict.

As we already established in Chapter 1, economics is about more than money alone. Although money is an important driver of economic behaviour, it is not the only one. Behavioural economists such as Daniel Kahneman argue that economic behaviour is also determined by individual experiences,[20] knowledge and psychosocial factors. Richard Thaler, the winner of the 2017

20   For many years, Daniel Kahneman worked with the psychologist Amos Tversky, writing on prospect theory. When making economic decisions, people's circumstances factor more in their decisions than the absolute expected gain;

Nobel Prize in Economics, even concludes on this basis that people's economic behaviour is 'irrational'. These ideas are also endorsed from a wellbeing standpoint, but we go further by proposing that economics is also about social, ecological and subjective values at multiple scale levels. The challenge is to link such a comprehensive and wide-ranging perspective to a suitable definition in economics.

Thus, the economy is not a closed, self-regulating system, despite our frequent tendency to think about economics in such terms.[21] In the end, it is not some kind of 'invisible hand', but people themselves who make decisions and steer economic processes and outcomes. In the remaining chapters, we will focus on *economic wellbeing*, because it is necessary to draw boundaries around economics as a science; economics cannot be about everything. 'Economic wellbeing' refers to the resources that are available to people and decisions about how they are used. When people have enough resources available to meet their needs and priorities, we can speak of economic wellbeing. When people do not have enough resources to meet their needs and priorities, we speak of economic deprivation or unfulfilled wellbeing. From a wellbeing perspective, there can be negative manifestations of material, relational and subjective wellbeing in the form of deprivation, poverty or exclusion, as well as positive manifestations.

Following the critical approach taken by Tony Lawson,[22] who has argued that economics as a science has become too far removed from people's daily experiences, I describe the economy in an ontological sense as a *social process* of human action in relation

losing weighs more heavily than winning. Source: Tversky and Kahneman 1974, 1981, 1992.

21   System thinking in economics is characterized by the attribution of one or more of the following characteristics to the economic system: uniformity, constancy in time and place, neutrality and closed-ness.

22   See the following publications by Tony Lawson: *Economics and Reality,* 1997 (Routledge); *Reorienting Economics,* 2003 (Routledge) and *Essays on the Nature and State of Modern Economics,* 2015 (Routledge).

to resources.[23] Below, inspired by the work of Tony Lawson, I introduce five axioms for a new Economics of Wellbeing.[24]

The economy is:

(i) an institutionalized process;
(ii) an open system;
(iii) structured and layered in accordance with temporary principles;
(iv) connected by internal relations;
(v) subject to emergent changes.

In the following sections, I explain these five axioms or basic principles in turn.

(i) The economy as an institutionalized allocation process

The first basic principle is that the economy is a socially and politically institutionalized process. This idea is derived from the thought of Karl Polanyi and later (heterodox) economists, including Tony Lawson, Edward Fullbrook, John Davis, Ben Fine, Edith Kuiper, Frederic Lee, Mark Lutz and Irene van Staveren. Following their ideas, in this book I define economics as an *institutionalized process of resource allocation by economic agents*. Allocation is understood as the consumption, production, distribution and co-creation of goods and services. As Douglas North put it in 1990, institutions comprise all formal and informal rules and norms that organize political and economic relations. The economy is embedded in a political system that itself forms part of a socio-cultural environment (society). Societies, in turn, are themselves embedded in physical and natural surroundings

23 'Ontology' refers to the doctrine of reality; in this context, the doctrine of economic reality, which addresses the philosophical question, 'what is economics'?
24 An axiom is a claim, accepted as a basic principle, which characterizes but does not prove a scientific theory, often in conjunction with a range of other axioms.

that have time- and context-specific qualities. This vision of economics as an institutionalized process is represented in Figure 3, in the form of four nested circles.[25] The size of these circles is not fixed; it is all about the relative picture. By making the economy the innermost circle, I simply wish to show that economics is embedded in a political, socio-cultural and natural environment. It does not mean that the economy lies at the heart of every research question; after all, this would depend on the research problem and the chosen scientific or disciplinary approach. However, economic problems do invariably lie at the heart of economic questions. By 'economic problem', I mean an *allocation* problem; in other words, how resources are used in the production, consumption, (re)distribution and co-creation of goods and services in an economy. In view of our key principle that the economy is institutionalized, it will be clear that solving an allocation problem is never a politically or socio-culturally neutral process (see also: Chang 2007). Moreover, there are implications for our natural surroundings. These implications can put more or less pressure on nature and the ability of its ecological processes to recover. In 2009, the Swedish physicist Johan Rockström and his research team at the Stockholm Resilience Centre developed the framework of the nine planetary boundaries, which indicate the sustainable limits of the human use of natural resources (such as ecosystem services). These planetary boundaries also influence one another. In her book on 'doughnut economics', Kate Raworth (2017) builds on this idea of planetary boundaries to show clearly how the economy must stay within certain limits if it is to be sustainable.

As economic agents, people are occupied with solving economic problems in relation to this complex environment every

25 I use the same figure in my introductory textbook on gender and wellbeing in microeconomics to explain that unequal gender relations also influence economic processes and outcomes. As 'gender' is socially constructed and, as such, a part and outcome of the broader socio-cultural surroundings, the link with 'economics' is clear. Source: N. Pouw (2017) *Introduction to Gender and Wellbeing in Microeconomics*, London and New York: Routledge.

Figure 3   The economy embedded in a political, socio-cultural and natural environment

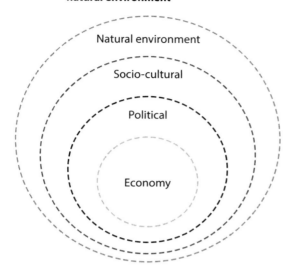

Natural environment

Socio-cultural

Political

Economy

Source: taken from Pouw (2017)

day. How do I divide my time between paid work and leisure? How can I get a permanent job? How can I feed my children? Should I invest in a degree or course, or would it be better to get a job and start earning money straight away? Where can I sell the tomatoes that I have grown on my land? Should I invest my savings in an equity fund or leave them in a low-interest savings account? Is it better to get solar panels for my roof or an electric car, or neither? The properties of and potential solutions to an economic problem are also determined by broader economic, political, socio-cultural and environmental factors. By defining the economy as an institutionalized process, I create the space that is needed to reveal the implicit and explicit operation of power relations in the economy. After all, power often works via institutions, which can undermine, reinforce or reproduce existing power relations. But at an individual and microlevel, too, it is important to pay attention to differences in power between economic agents. Power co-determines economic processes, policy and outcomes. When analysing economic behaviour, it is crucial to show how economic decisions are partly informed by someone's position, social and political identity, resources, relations and sphere of influence within politics, in society and in their everyday surroundings.

(ii) The economy is open to influences from the 'outside'

Based on the insight that the economy is an institutionalized process, not a closed and verifiable system, we can subsequently argue that economic processes and outcomes are influenced by power relations between economic agents at every scale level. Some of these power relations are perpetuated by legislation, treaties, behavioural rules (written and unwritten) and provisions. In this way, power is implicitly and explicitly 'institutionalized' by social and economic institutions.[26] However, power relations are often more deeply embedded in historical cultural values and norms, customs and convictions, and implicitly shape economic decision-making, allocation processes and outcomes. Tony Lawson explains this point in his work on the socio-cultural institutionalization of economics (1994, 1997, 2003). The economy is thereby open to influences from the 'outside', including socio-cultural, political and environmental conditions and changes. The exchange of goods and services between economic agents is not only achieved through relative prices and markets where supply meets demand, but also through power relations; for example, the power to access to a supply market of goods and

26 Within economic science, there are two movements that standardly take the role of institutions into account in economic analysis, by means of transaction costs and information costs: (1) Institutional Economics, with an emphasis on formal institutions (e.g., governments and courts). Thorstein Veblen is considered a key founding father of this movement. (2) New Institutional Economics (NIE), which emphasizes social legal norms and rules. Ronald Coase and Douglas North and Olliver E. Williamson are key founders of the NIE.

services at all, the power to communicate with a potential user of goods and services, or the power to gather knowledge or information about prices and customer preferences. In fact, power relations are more fundamental than prices and markets; power shapes the exchange of goods and services that only becomes apparent through neutral factors such as prices and markets. For example, a small South African farmer has less negotiating power to ask an attractive sales price for his crops when he lacks transport to sell them at the town's market, with its higher prices, and is instead dependent on buyers who stop by from time to time to buy crops at a lower price. Power becomes vulnerable to abuse when political and economic interests are interwoven.

Power magnifies all kinds of forms of economic inequality: unequal remuneration for the same kind of work, unequal access to credit or subsidies due to underlying conditions, unequal access to social, business and political networks. What applies to power relations also applies to cultural and social customs, laws and codes of conduct; these (non-neutral) factors shape the economic process of allocating and exchanging goods and servi-ces. In the Netherlands until 1973, for example, the government allowed employers to dismiss women when they got married. This meant that women could not keep working, or could only keep working in secret, with all the negative consequences this had for pay and promotion. In addition, socio-cultural practices or rules relating to common resources can influence how they are used and exchanged (e.g., drinking water, oxygen, forests, fossil fuels, ecosystem services). For example, many fishing communities in Southern India follow the unwritten collective rule that there is less fishing in low season, to give the young fish a chance to grow and allow stocks recover after a period of intensive fishing in high season. In this way, small fishing communities succeeded for centuries in fishing within the limits of sustainability, until the advent of overfishing, political and economic conflicts about fishing grounds at sea, and confron-tation with large-scale fishing companies. *Vice versa*, economic processes also influence the political, socio-cultural and natural environment by demanding (new) regulations, influencing socio-cultural intercourse, and investing (or disinvesting) in social equality or sustainability. In short, the economy is an open system that influences people's political, socio-cultural and environmental surroundings, and is itself influenced by them. These open connections are represented visually by the dotted lines in Figure 3 above. Despite this, economics as an institutionalized process can in essence be distinguished from the political, socio-cultural and natural domain, because it focuses on *the institutionalized process of resource allocation* as a research object, with *economic agents* that make decisions about this as its subject. Nature is conditional on every economic process, but it is not in itself an economic agent, because it has no self-determination. Nature has instrumental and intrinsic value for human wellbeing. When striving to optimize collective wellbeing, it is therefore important to take care of nature and its ecosystems.

(iii) The economy is structured and layered

The economy as a social process is open to influences from the 'outside', but it is simultaneously organized in accordance with certain structures and layers (levels). These structures and layers are temporal: they can change over time, although they can be seen as 'constants' over long periods. 'Economic structure' refers to the organization of an economy around economic agents, institutions and sectors. 'Layered' refers to the different levels in the economy at which aggregation and measurement of economic indicators take place. These structures and layers influence the categories of economic agents that are the subject of economic analysis, such as individuals, households, associations, businesses, the government and semi-governmental organizations. We also see these categories reflected in economic models, theories and measurement instruments. For example, national accounts – a key economic planning instrument – are organized in accordance with the categories of households and businesses at the microlevel, sectors and government at the macrolevel, and everything that is abroad at the international level.

The national accounts are linked to economic models, procedures and monetary units, and also have the tendency to be fixed for long periods. This is because they are deeply embedded in the working methods of economic planners and statisticians; their expertise, methods and statistical indicators. It would not be feasible to change the calculation method every year, as this would complicate making comparisons over time. The national accounts are a key instrument used by Statistics Netherlands to calculate all revenue and expenditure flows in the Dutch economy, and to use these to make forecasts about future economic scenarios. The United Nations' System of National Accounts (SNA) sets out the standard that must be met by countries' national accounts. In addition, within the SNA framework, European countries must also adhere to the European System of Integrated National Accounts (ESA). In accordance with these institutionalized structures, work-forms and categories, knowledge about the economy is produced and reproduced in the form of economic indicators and structured data sets. Economic categories are therefore an important starting point for economic analysis and measurement. Gross Domestic Product (GNP), for example, is a measurement of the total added value of all goods and services produced in a national economy. GNP is thus an indicator that is closely linked to the production of goods and services in the paid economy, but it does not tell us anything about the added value of the unpaid economy and the contribution made by nature. That said, attempts are being made to attribute a monetary value to certain aspects of domestic work and voluntary work and to discount the use of ecosystem services, and to include both in the national accounts. These are slow-moving processes, however, that require the endorsement and cooperation of multiple countries and agencies. They are preceded by many debates and research studies at different scale levels. Since 2007, for example, in the 'Beyond GDP' initiative,[27] the European Commission has been working with the European Parliament, the OECD and the World Wildlife Fund to research the development of alternative indicators for social progression and sustainability, which can ultimately be linked to national accounts. What should be noted, in any case, is that economic categories never need to be the end-point of analysis and theory formation, and new indicators, categories and structures can become relevant over time. We should therefore keep developing new measures and indicators as instruments for up-to-date economic analysis (see further Chapter 9).

(iv) The economy is connected by internal relations

The economy is characterized by internal relations between economic agents on the one hand, and the resources they produce, consume and distribute on the other; and there are internal connections between them. In economics, production, consumption and distribution are summarized as 'allocation'. Allocation is an active concept; without allocation, the economy would grind to a halt, as it were. Allocation is also a binding concept; it connects economic agents and economic processes with one another. According to neoclassical economic theory, allocation takes place based on the mutual relationship between the demand for and supply of paid goods and services in the private sector. Because there is demand for oil, oil is exploited; because there is a supply of a new kind of telephone, demand emerges. According to this theory, the relationship between market demand and supply is expressed in relative prices. The relative price is the relationship

27 The European 'Beyond GDP' initiative began in 2007 with an international conference of the same name. Since then, various research reports and strategic surveys have been published. For more information, see: http://ec.europa.eu/ environment/beyond_gdp/background_en.html

between the price of two goods or services. Supply and demand are brought together in the market by an 'invisible hand'. If the demand for goods or services increases relative to supply, the price usually rises, assuming that this price is not controlled and is 'free' to move. If demand falls relative to supply, the price falls. Market exchange between economic agents is thus an important driver (mechanism) of allocation in the private sector, and is grounded in the relationship between the demand for and supply of paid goods and services. Market exchange allows people to purchase and sell resources in line with their desires, needs and opportunities. Assuming that prices are not regulated, relative prices reflect the relationship between demand and supply. By means of exchange, people can provide for, improve and enrich their circumstances, and seize opportunities to increase their wellbeing.

The idea that demand and supply are brought together by an 'invisible hand' is nonsensical; it obscures the fact that people with the power to access resources can organize and steer supply and demand. People who lack power cannot do this, and usually experience the 'invisible hand' of the market as something that works against them; it excludes them from participating, because they cannot meet the applicable market conditions or because they simply lack access. However, aside from dictatorial rule by absolute sovereigns (people, organizations and states), a large part of economic allocation in the world takes place in accordance with other mechanisms. Some of these mechanisms are typical of particular economic domains. Market exchange, for example, is a typical driver in the private sector, and redistribution is typical in the public sector. However, these characteristic mechanisms within domains do not preclude other mechanisms. There can also be gifts and favours in the private sector, or a certain degree of redistribution based on principles of equality. A certain amount of market exchange can also take place in the public sector, for example to (partially) fund public services such as libraries and schools. The domains and typical mechanisms are listed below and represented in Figure 4:

[1] Individuals & households & social groups and communities -> *reciprocity and support (flourishing, aspiration, pursuit of individual and shared life goals)*

In the unpaid economic domain, individuals, households and social groups and communities (e.g., neighbourhood associations) allocate resources for the production, consumption and redistribution of goods and services. The dominant driver of the allocation between these agents is reciprocity and/or support. The exchange of goods and services is based on personal relations, which are exchanged for nothing but a possible gift or favour in return (now or in future). Parents care for their children and may (or may not) expect similar in return, for example in the form of care in their old age. Nothing is fixed, though, as there is no contract or formal agreement; at most, there is a social or moral obligation to give something in return. Reciprocity can contribute to wellbeing in a positive or negative way; family support can give someone a great sense of self-confidence and stability, but it can also be experienced as an onerous obligation in the form of (overly) high expectations. In extended families in many African countries, for example, it is customary for a family member who has been successful, in the eyes of their relatives, to be expected to give broad financial support to a number of cousins; for example, paying their school fees and enabling them to do further study, or covering medical bills. It is not always possible to meet these financial expectations, which can lead to stress and conflict between relatives.

[2] Private sector (national and international businesses and organizations) -> *market exchange (good quality of life, better quality of life thanks to creation of opportunities to improve wellbeing)*

In the private sector, entrepreneurs, businesses and organizations use market exchange to allocate goods and services. The market is defined as a physical or virtual space where the exchange of goods and services takes place between economic agents, for payment in money, goods or services. This exchange is not conditional on personal relationships; it can be completely anonymous, as in the case of shares and bond markets, for example. If there is a free market, and there are no monopolies (price-fixing) or subsidies (price-subsidizing), the eventual price is determined by supply and demand. When supply is greater than demand, this leads to lower prices; when demand is greater than supply, this leads to higher prices. Money is a means of exchange and facilitates impersonal exchange, but that is not to say that all market exchange is impersonal. Market exchange can also be partly grounded in personal or shared relationships: a neighbourhood resident's desire to shop exclusively at local stores, for example, or remain loyal to a particular brand or family business. Some of the world's cultural communities still use a traditional barter economy where no money changes hands, but goods and services are instead exchanged for other goods and services. For example, two chickens might be exchanged for a sack of grain. New forms of barter economy are also developing across the world, in which people exchange services, for example; a haircut in exchange for an odd job at home, or a cooked meal in exchange for babysitting. These new mechanisms for bypassing the market, as it were, are emerging at a time when people are seeking more personal contact and community spirit, and do not want to see themselves reduced to being purely impersonal 'consumers'.

[3] Public sector (national and international governments and semi-governmental agencies) -> *redistribution (living together well by sharing wellbeing)*

In the public sector, which consists of the government and semi-governmental agencies, redistribution is the primary driver of allocation. Local and national governments collect taxes, generate revenue (without profit) for government services and provisions, or earn interest on their possessions (e.g., property). These resources are used to finance the government apparatus, but also for redistribution, through the supply of public goods and services such as clean drinking water, infrastructure, legal and judicial organs, health institutions, refugee aid, schools and hospitals. The degree of redistribution is highly dependent on the political-economic system in question. The Netherlands and Scandinavian countries have relatively high levels of income taxation and a high level of redistribution, for example, something that is much less evident in the United Kingdom and the United States. Opinions about this are rooted in social ideas about distribution, wellbeing and justice. For example, a national government might want to support its farmers by putting export subsidies on frozen chicken meat from African countries such as Ghana and the Ivory Coast. The Dutch government uses such subsidies, for example, as do the Brazilian, American and many other European governments, which attach high value to maintaining their agricultural sectors. This can create unfair competition for small local farmers, and even price them out of the market. Secondary effects such as these are not always predicted or considered to be important. Each time we must therefore ask ourselves: *'Who stands to gain from this redistribution?'* Another example is the public provision of education and healthcare. When these are high-quality services and available to all for an affordable fee, this can lead to a large-scale redistribution of opportunities (in a positive sense), whereby the chance of getting a good education or good healthcare is independent of one's income or political power. Government subsidies can also be used to provide services and provisions in locations that are not served by the market, because this is not sufficiently interesting from a cost-benefit perspective. Take, for example, a bus service in an isolated village. Such a service is not cost-effective if it is only considered from a profit perspective, but when viewed from a human wellbeing perspective, it can have a great impact on the mobility and freedom of the village residents.

We can also identify hybrid partnerships, including new economic phenomena and combinations of allocation mechanisms:

[4] Hybrid partnerships, such as public-private partnerships (PPPs), prosumers,[28] and economic platforms[29] -> *co-creation* (*any combination of two or all of the mechanisms above*)

In the domain of hybrid partnerships, which consist of representatives of two or three of the above-mentioned domains/sectors, co-creation drives resource allocation. Co-creation is generally understood to mean a form of cooperation in which all participants influence the creative process and its outcomes, such as a joint neighbourhood security scheme, advice, or a product (e.g., crowdsourcing, social media advice, or test-laboratories where a business develops new product tastes in collaboration with consumers). Participants in co-creation have a shared interest, but they can also pursue their own interests, which is what makes them different from other participants. With the aid of modern communication aids, especially digital platforms, various participants are managing to connect increasingly quickly. Forms of collaboration can emerge with different combinations of economic agents. Public-private partnerships (PPPs) are a form of collaboration that is occurring more and more frequently, leading to co-creation in the economy. When co-creation becomes the most important allocation mechanism in an economy, we can speak of a transformation of that economy; the economy then starts to function on the basis of different mechanisms and relationships.

These four mechanisms of economic allocation can be typical of certain economic domains, sectors or forms of collaboration (Figure 4), but they are certainly not the only allocation mechanisms. There are also countless intermediary forms. For example, many digital platforms in the private sector are driven more by market exchange between suppliers and users (e.g., the taxi

28 *Prosumers* are consumers who have a significant stake in the realization of a product or service that they themselves (partly) consume.
29 *Platforms* in the economy are forms of cooperation that co-create goods and services by making use of digital networks and user platforms.

Figure 4   Dominant allocation mechanisms in the economy

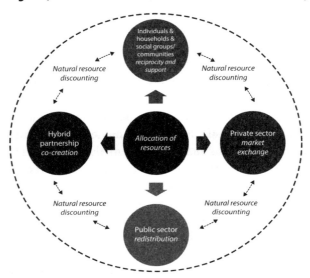

Source: adapted from Pouw and McGregor 2014

platform Uber or the food delivery website Thuisbezorgd.nl) than by co-creation, if at all. When it comes to the exchange of goods and services, we can think of numerous other mechanisms, such as individual habits and social conventions, 'copycat behaviour' (e.g., 'keeping up with the Joneses'), cultural customs and norms, altruism, exploitation, theft, coercion and deception. Slavery, forced child labour, racism, discrimination and exclusion are all examples of social systems that produce unequal and involuntary allocation mechanisms. These are ultimately unsustainable, due to their destructive impact on humans and life. Nevertheless, these allocation mechanisms can exist for long periods.

Finally, there is a fifth allocation mechanism that is not fully recognized in economic science at present: that of natural resource discounting. In Figure 4, this is represented by the dotted circle around the entire system.

[5] All economic agents make use of nature in the form of eco-system services, biodiversity and landscape -> *extraction of natural resources in combination with gifts, market exchange, redistribution and co-creation, which must be accompanied by discounting*

All economic agents make use of natural resources and space in economic allocation processes. Natural resources and space are allocated through the free use of nature, market exchange, redistribution and co-creation. This fifth mechanism should be built into every economic model as a matter of course. In Chapter 8, I explain why this is crucial from a sustainability perspective.

(v) The economy is characterized by emergent properties

For the most part, the aim of economic analysis is to make predictions about future trends or outcomes. Making accurate predictions helps us to draw up economic plans, but making such predictions is by no means easy. Even with the aid of the most advanced computational models, it is difficult to foresee the economic future. There are four reasons for this.

First, every economic model is based on knowledge about the past. The factors that are taken into account in a model as *endogenous* variables may be able to explain economic growth well over the last ten years, but they are not necessarily the same variables that will explain future economic growth. 'Endogenous' refers to a change or shock in an economic outcome variable (the dependent variable) that emerges within an economic model (and is thus explained by a series of independent variables, such as x_1, $x_2 \ldots x_{10}$). Future growth, meanwhile, may well be explained by variables that were *exogenous* to the previous model (for example, x_{11}, x_{12} and x_{13}). 'Exogenous' means that the change or shock comes from outside the economic model.

Second, the mutual relations between endogenous variables in an economic model can change over time under the influence of exogenous variables, uncertainty, and/or due to feedback mechanisms and anticipatory behaviour by economic agents. Although this makes economic analysis less linear, it does more justice to the increased links between economic domains (sectors, households and social communities) resulting from globalization and increasing communication and mobility.

Third, many economic models overlook the heterogeneity of economic agents, and are blind to the entanglement of economic agents in pluriform economic domains. For example, the decision to get a new job is not only made on the basis of salary considerations or the content of the work and career opportunities, but also location, work-life balance, and factors relating to one's social community (for example, the religion, social group or class to which someone does/does not want to belong). Economic agents make complex trade-offs between the three dimensions of wellbeing (material, relational and subjective – see Figure 2), between individual and collective wellbeing, and between past, present and future wellbeing. The behaviour of economic agents is thus not only determined by trade-offs in the market domain,[30] but also interwoven with their simultaneous role as economic actors in other domains (households, social communities). An economic decision made in one domain (for example, relating to resources or time) has a direct influence on economic decision-making in another domain of the *same* economic agent. In economic analysis, these domains and economic agents are considered in isolation from one another, as though they did not concern one and the same person. In reality, however, people are economic agents in several domains simultaneously (household, paid work, member of a community).

Fourth, when aggregating from micro- from macro-economic processes, the nature and meaning of these same processes

---

30   This is a point of criticism that relates to the androcentric tendency that has shaped economic science (and other fields of science) for centuries. This is what motivated me to study economics, and later to write my book *Introduction to Gender and Wellbeing in Microeconomics* (Routledge, 2017).

change. In other words, qualitative changes (transformations) can take place in the process of aggregating (see explanation in Chapter 2). Collective wellbeing as a whole can thus be larger or smaller than the sum of its parts, as a result of synergetic (or undermining) effects. For example, planting new trees at the local level may not solve the problem of air pollution, but if trees are planted in several locations, this may create synergy and solve the pollution problem.

Each of the four above-mentioned causes can led to unexpected economic changes, turning points and shocks, which can be built into an economic model as 'emergent properties'. This leads to scenario-like exercises and predictions based on (different versions of) an economic model, rather than a point estimate. I would thus urge economic researchers to put much more energy into developing and calculating alternative scenarios, and to collaborate on this with other social and natural scientists, in order to take account of these various complexities. Inter-disciplinary collaboration is important for economists when attempting to solve the age-old economic puzzle of how to translate microeconomic processes into macroeconomic processes and outcomes (and *vice versa*), even if only approximately.

5 The Wellbeing Economics Matrix (WEM)

The five axioms of the new 'Wellbeing Economics', introduced in Chapter 4, form the building blocks for a pluralistic vision of economics with wellbeing, human-human relations and human-nature interaction at its core. They also form the ontological starting points for a new framework for analysing Wellbeing Economics. Collective wellbeing, rather than economic growth alone, has become the most important measure of a successful economy. For this purpose, this chapter introduces the Wellbeing Economics Matrix (WEM) (original source: Pouw and McGregor 2014). This matrix resembles a social accounting matrix (SAM),[31] which is used in practice by economic planners and statisticians to measure all money flows for the exchange of goods and services between economic agents in a national economy. It is linked to the System of National Accounts (SNA), because it uses the same definitions and categories of economic agents (macro-identities) on the production and consumption sides. All of these economic agents form part of the economic cycle. Statistical agencies use SAMs when making economic predictions based on budgets; for example, about the growth in Gross National Product (GNP) for a certain budget allocation. Although the WEM is a theoretical idea that needs further technical development before it can be used in practice, it does offer a fundamental and robust starting point for systematically charting material and non-material economic exchange between economic agents and nature. As in

---

31   In the 1970s, Erik Thorbecke and Graham Pyatt (one of my first mentors) carried out fundamental research to make the social accounting matrix technically useable as an economic planning instrument, and promoted its use at the World Bank. Graham Pyatt had previously worked for the Cambridge Growth Project under Richard Stone (1913-1991) and Alan Brown (1928-2010), who developed the very first SAM in 1962. In 1984, Richard Stone was awarded the Nobel Prize in Economics for his key contribution to input-output analysis in economic accounting.

a SAM, all economic agents appear in the WEM twice, as input for the matrix rows and columns. After all, economic agents can provide goods and services as producers *and* receive them as consumers.[32] The number of rows is thus by definition equal to the number of columns. 'Nature' has also been included in the economic cycle of the WEM, despite being difficult to describe as an 'economic agent'.

In short, the WEM (Table 2) differs from a traditional SAM in terms of its:

(i)   multi-dimensionality;
(ii)   categories of economic agents;
(iii)   types of goods and services;
(iv)   types of flows;
(v)   filled-in diagonal;
(vi)   instrumental and intrinsic connections with nature.

I shall explain each of these differences in turn. First, the WEM forms the prelude to a multi-dimensional economic analysis based on objective or subjective values,[33] or both. This is linked to the type of 'transactions' that are registered by the WEM. Rather than 'transactions', I prefer to use the term 'exchange', because the exchange of goods and services does not always involve money (take, for instance, unpaid domestic work, voluntary work, or some uses of ecosystem services). Whereas the analytical framework of a SAM only registers money flows, the WEM has three dimensions/layers: (1) a material WEM1 based on monetary exchange (similar to the SAM, but including paid

---

32   This also indicates the limitation of the WEM. In Chapter 4, Figure 4, I mentioned the emergence of co-creation as a driver of economic allocation, whereby the dividing line between producers and consumers is becoming blurred. There is still no prosumer category in the SAM and the WEM.

33   As economic variables are not always purely objective or purely subjective, I nuance this with 'more'. According to Amartya Sen, economic analysis can at most claim 'positional objectivity', because a subjective choice lies at the root of every economic variable, due to the selection or definition of this variable (source: Amaratya Sen, 1993, 'Positional Objectivity').

and unpaid goods and services); (2) a relational WEM2 based on the economic relations that are needed in order to facilitate exchange; and (3) a subjective WEM3 based on value judgements about (the pursued or realized) WEM1 and WEM2 (see Figure 5).

Together, these three WEMS can be aggregated into 'collective wellbeing' – the closing entry of the matrix in Table 2 – but they cannot be aggregated on a single scale, because they are based on different underlying scales (objective and subjective) and consider different forms of exchange (material and relational). However, these three WEMs are connected to one another in space and time, which is why the WEM is described as 'layered'. We will thus need to analyse the complete WEM using different methods, namely by looking at the point intersections and connections between the three layers of the WEM. In Chapter 6, on the Implications for Methodology, I shall discuss the analysis of point intersections and interconnectedness in this layered matrix in more detail.

Second, the WEM distinguishes two more types of economic agent than the traditional SAM. Whereas in a SAM, 'households' are categorized as the primary economic agent, the WEM distinguishes between 'individuals' and 'households', because goods and services are also exchanged between households themselves (inside and outside households). When the consumption and production of goods and services is aggregated at the household level, redistribution and exchange – and consequently any inequalities – remain invisible *within* households. This does introduce the accounting complication that individuals within a household share some goods and services, creating economies of scale as a result. However, it is relatively simple to correct for this complication with a reduction factor for the total value of shared goods and services within a household. The advantage of this – making economic inequalities within households visible – outweighs the disadvantage of introducing the accounting complication. In addition, the WEM identifies 'social groups and communities' as an economic agent, a category that does not appear in the SAM. Examples of such social groups

Figure 5 The three layers of the Wellbeing Economics Matrix (WEM)

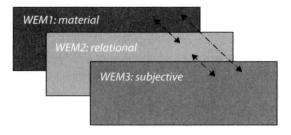

and communities include sports associations, professional and lobbying associations, neighbourhood associations, voluntary organizations, political organizations, environmental movements, religious and civil society organizations, and so forth. These were already mentioned in relation to the allocation mechanisms in Chapter 4, Figure 4. 'Reciprocity and support' were mentioned as the most important drivers of the exchange of goods and services between members of social groups and communities. Although social groups and communities are not usually seen as 'economic agents', they do participate in economic exchange to be able to carry out their activities. Social groups and communities can form important networks of relations that allow people to access and control resources in the economy; for example, belonging to a professional network can increase one's access to certain jobs. In a positive sense, social groups and communities can increase social cohesion; in a negative sense, they can lead to exclusion and discrimination. Social groups and communities produce and consume goods and services, and they sometimes receive them, too (due to a government subsidy, for example). Many of these goods and services are not exchanged via the market, nor are they necessarily in line with prevailing market value, meaning that they partly fall outside the national accounting system. There are different power relations between people within social groups and communities, which can lead to unequal resource allocation.

Third, the WEM provides a framework for registering paid *and* unpaid goods and services in the economy. The latter include unpaid domestic goods and services, voluntary work, and the use of ecosystem services. In satellite accounts in national accounting systems, various countries are already experimenting with calculating the economic value of unpaid labour, natural resources and environmental costs. In most cases, an alternative market value is attached to these goods and services, based on input (labour) or output value. Only when international agreement is reached on the standard method for this will changes be made to the international SNA. For now, we can only imagine the wealth of insights that would be gained into the quality of economic development and growth if the actual use of unpaid labour, voluntary work and ecosystem services were to be made visible. This would be a minimal first step in the direction of sustainable and more inclusive policy – although a lack of political resolution is the greatest delaying factor at present.

Fourth, and as a consequence of the inclusion of social groups and communities, the WEM also provides an opportunity to consider the economic relations and networks that form the preconditions for economic exchange. These can be relations and networks in the paid and unpaid economies, also described in the literature as 'social capital' (see Robert Putnam's groundbreaking research on social capital in American society from 2001).

Fifth, I argue that the WEM should be used differently for economic analysis and planning. Whereas the diagonal of the SAM is normally left empty, I argue that the diagonal should be used pro-actively in order to provide insight *ex ante* into wellbeing differences and trade-offs between (groups of) economic agents and dimensions of wellbeing, instead of *ex post* and *ad hoc* (for example, in response to parliamentary questions). This point will be further developed in Chapter 7, 'A Focus on Inequality'. In this way, the WEM offers a holistic framework for analysing economic exchange and how this contributes to wellbeing. The WEM thereby not only offers insight into exchange in the paid economy, but also in the unpaid economy and the use of ecosystem services, which are not otherwise covered in national accounts. In the following, I give a detailed explanation of the variables and functions specified in the WEM (Table 2). The WEM differentiates between 'individuals' (I) and 'households' (H), and identifies 'social groups and communities' (C) as economic agents, in addition to firms (businesses and entrepreneurs), 'government' (G) and 'the rest of the world' (W). The matrix ends with 'net savings' (S) and 'net investments' (N). Net savings and investments connect the process of economic wellbeing in the present with that in the past and future. The WEM is read from column (provider) to row (receiver). The goods and services that are exchanged between providers and receivers can protect, maintain or improve wellbeing in a positive sense, or undermine or nullify it in a negative sense. This is possible in a material sense (M), in a relational sense (R), and/or in a subjective sense (S). The nature, strength and sign (+ or -) of these relations is expressed in functional form (F) and is based on empirical data in practice.

Finally, the sixth difference from the SAM is that the WEM recognizes the instrumental *and* intrinsic interconnectedness between economic processes and nature. Natural resources and space are of *instrumental* importance to economic production and consumption. The raw materials industry is based on the extraction of coal, bauxite and minerals from mines. The use of forests, agricultural land and fishing grounds forms a basis for the existence of the world's population, and an immediate basis for many communities' livelihoods. If bees were to disappear, humans would lose many sources of food, and we have yet to start on clean drinking water, air and solar energy. The amount of material and energy that can be extracted from nature in order to facilitate economic processes is limited. Kate Raworth represents this principle visually with the outer rim of her 'doughnut economy' (Raworth 2017). In addition, nature is an *intrinsic source* of inspiration, mental health and spiritual wellbeing, and biotic and abiotic processes make people aware of their own qualities as natural beings. It can also bind groups of people and social processes. As human beings, we can recharge and recover by being in nature, or become aware of our own development and mortality. In this way, nature also has intrinsic value for human wellbeing. As such, nature is a precondition for human wellbeing and the economic processes that produce individual and collective wellbeing. In a negative sense, nature can also threaten and undermine human wellbeing. Natural disasters threaten the human species on a large scale, as was shown last year (2019) by the extensive flooding in Zimbabwe, Mozambique and Malawi, and the massive forest fires in Australia. Human interconnectedness with nature could thus be described as ambivalent; we are part of nature and dependent on it, but nature can also be our enemy. Although nature is not an 'economic agent', because it is all-encompassing, I have deliberately made the exchange between economic activities and nature visible from a Wellbeing Economics perspective (see row and column 7 in the WEM, Table 2). Nature conservation, the prevention of environmental pollution, and investing in natural recovery are all wise investments from a wellbeing standpoint. After all, we cannot survive without nature. But the construction of dikes, technologies for controlling flood management and earthquake-resistant infrastructure are also wise investments from a Wellbeing Economics perspective, because humanity must be able to protect itself from nature and a changing climate, both now and in the future.

Thus, on the one hand, people are dependent on nature in an instrumental and intrinsic sense; there can be no life on Earth without nature. On the other hand, nature forms a threat to humanity and we have to protect ourselves against it; for example, against flooding, drought, earthquakes, extreme heat and cold, animals, and so forth. Nature, in turn, is protected and can recover thanks to human investments in nature. On the other hand, humans deplete natural resources as a result of the way we live. Figure 6 shows this reciprocal relationship between human wellbeing and nature.

To gain more insight into how the WEM works (Table 2), I develop two examples below. These examples discuss positive contributions to wellbeing, but it should be remembered that such relations can also be negative or neutral. First, we start by

Figure 6 The reciprocal relationship between wellbeing and nature

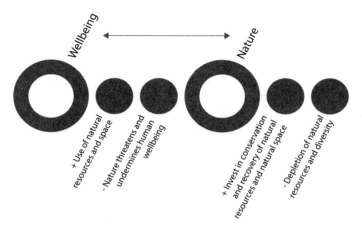

reading the matrix input in column 1 and row 2, to see which unpaid goods and services the individual (I) provides to the household (*subscript h*) in the form of I_h. These can include: goods and services that contribute to the material wellbeing of the household (M_i) in the form of income, a legacy or sustainable assets; goods and services that contribute to relational wellbeing (R_i) in the form of social capital and the relationship between humans and nature; and goods and services that contribute to the subjective wellbeing of the household (S_i), for example in the form of happiness, satisfaction or certain cultural values and norms. This multi-dimensional relationship between the individual and the household is specified by the function F_h. This function refers to a sub-matrix consisting of three different interrelationships between the three dimensions of wellbeing. The value of the individual contribution to the *material wellbeing* (M_i) of the household is positive if $M_i > 0$, negative if $M_i < 0$ and neutral if $M_i = 0$. This value is measured on a monetary scale (as in a SAM). The value of the individual contribution to the *relational wellbeing* (R_i) of the household is measured on a non-monetary scale. The value of social capital and the relationship between humans and nature are difficult to express in monetary terms. They can be measured quantitatively, however, for example by counting the number of different types of relations (social capital),[34] or in terms of a sustainability indicator, such as the ecological footprint or the amount of carbon emissions. Depending on which set of indicators is chosen, R_i can assume positive and negative values. If the aim is to aggregate and to make interpersonal and household comparisons, it is naturally important to choose an unambiguous measurement method. Finally, the individual provides goods and services that can contribute to the subjective wellbeing of the household, shown by S_i. Because this involves subjective data, it is difficult or even undesirable to measure the value. Subjective data can be translated into priorities (rankings of values), however, or we can again use a Likert scale, which provides an approximate measurement for a fixed qualitative indicator. For example, Likert scales can be used to measure subjective values such as 'trust', 'happiness' or 'cohesion'. *Vice versa*, when I_h is mirrored in the diagonal axis of the matrix, we can see what individuals receive in the form of unpaid goods and services from the household to which they belong, indicated by H_i (column 2, row 1). The household provides accommodation and shared meals that contribute to the material wellbeing of its individual members (M_h). In a relational sense, the household also provides family ties and access to other social capital, all of which contributes to individual relational wellbeing (R_h). Finally, the household offers a sense of security, personal fulfilment and meaning, in the form of subjective wellbeing (Sh). The function F_i then shows the sub-matrix that consists of the previous three interrelations of individual wellbeing.

A second example considers the exchange of goods and services between firms (F_c) and social groups and communities. The

34 In the literature on social capital, a distinction is usually made between 'bonding' social capital (between members of a group who share some common characteristic), 'bridging' social capital (when social groups connect with other groups) and 'linking' social capital (connecting with groups and institutions that have relative power). Sources: Robert Putnam (2000) and Simon Szreter (2002).

matrix input for this can be found in column 3, row 4. The firm provides employment and economic activity for a community of people. This contributes to the material wellbeing of the community, which is shown by (M_f). The firm undertakes its economic activities in a way that has an impact on the natural environment, for example by emitting CO_2, in the case of a factory, or through the extraction of natural resources. This relationship is indicated with (R_f). Finally, the firm provides its employees with future prospects and a sense of identity in the community, as shown by (S_f). This explains why a community can feel abandoned when a large company leaves in order to establish itself elsewhere. The nature, strength and sign (+ or -) of the relationships above is again shown in functional form with F_c, consisting of a sub-matrix of the above-mentioned three interrelationships of wellbeing. *Vice versa*, if F_c is mirrored in the diagonal, we can analyse the exchange of goods and services from a social community to the firm, using C_f(column 4, row 3). The community provides the firm with physical space and proximity to infrastructure, all of which contributes to the firm's income and profits (M_c). The community also offers a pool of labour to the professional and social networks that contribute to the firm's public relations (R_c). Finally, the proximity and activities of the firm can generate goodwill (or ill-will) in the community (S_c). In this case, the function C_f represents the sub-matrix of the above-mentioned three interrelationships of wellbeing.

From these examples, we can draw the following interim conclusions about the potential application of the WEM in empirical analysis:

(1) As the framework must satisfy the condition of robustness, every column corresponds to a row, and the whole is aggregated into the last cell on the diagonal.

(2) Three versions/dimensions of the WEM can be derived from this one WEM (Table 2): the material WEM1, the relational WEM2 and the subjective WEM3. This goes back to the basic principle that 'wellbeing' is three-dimensional. The three dimensions of wellbeing can be analysed *collectively*

by means of intersections (or cross-sections), indicated by the symbol ∩.

(3) The rows and columns are aggregated at different levels (agents, micro and macro) into collective wellbeing, using the unit functions (U). The unit function is used to show that it is the *crossing-points* that fall within the different intersections when observations are measured.

(4) The WEM can thus be analysed in terms of (more) objective and subjective values, and subjective values that have been made objective (using rankings and Likert scales).

(5) At present, it is probably only possible to combine the quantifiable relations of the WEM (WEM1) with the SNA. However, this does not apply to the three additional categories: individuals, social groups and communities, and nature (see further Chapter 6, 'Implications for Methodology').

A number of specific points should be made with regard to 'rest of the world' (W) and 'net investments' (N) and 'net savings' (SV), which are also included in the WEM. By 'rest of the world' is meant, in a material sense, the trade balance – the value of exported goods and services minus imports; in a relational sense, foreign relations (e.g., membership of the EU, UN, diplomatic corps) and the sustainability of these; and in a subjective sense, the perception of the rest of the world and a national economy's position in the world (e.g., in terms of international goodwill, trust and security). The economic activities and wellbeing of individuals, households, firms, social groups and communities and the government are influenced, directly or indirectly, by the 'rest of the world'. For example, Dutch membership of the EU confers on Dutch citizens the benefit of travelling freely to EU countries; it offers companies certain trade and fiscal advantages; and it gives the government access to subsidies and support. On the other hand, this is offset by the considerable cost of EU membership contributions. In a relational sense, it gives access to other social groups and communities in the EU, and in a subjective sense, it provides a certain identity or sense of security. 'Net investments' can refer to material investments (money, gold or other sustainable investments), investments in social capital or sustainability, and, from a subjective perspective, the construction of positive value judgements about this on a collective scale (e.g., public opinion). Net investments not only relate to money, but they can also relate to investment in time, or investment in social relationships based on trust. All economic agents make such 'net investments' or 'net savings', measured over a certain period of time. 'Net savings' can refer to material savings (e.g., money in a savings account), savings on social capital and sustainability, and, in a subjective sense, through negative value judgements (e.g., through negative publicity and public opinion regarding a product or firm). Wellbeing is not only an outcome, but it is also a process; in the economic allocation process, people choose between different forms of economic production, consumption and distribution. The relations (social and with nature) and subjectivities that are associated with this cannot be viewed in isolation from the material economy.

As a coherent analytical framework for 'Wellbeing Economics', the WEM matrix represents a fundamental step in the operationalization of the theory. I consider this necessary before taking further steps towards the functional development of this complex framework, because it is the only way to ensure the robustness of this pluralistic approach. The greatest challenge of the scheme is to integrate the objective and subjective values. For now, it is sufficient to conclude that the three-dimensional WEM provides space for innovative economic analysis, paying attention to the non-monetary exchange of goods and services (including unpaid labour and ecological indicators), and subjective values and standards that denote meaning. Although we can attribute numbers to the latter in order to make them quantifiable in economic analysis, in essence they continue to represent qualitative values and standards.

With the aid of the comprehensive WEM framework, new questions and concepts can be developed and new economic relationships investigated in a robust way, such as those between the paid and unpaid economies, between nature and human well-being, and between material money flows and social networks, and subjective perceptions of both. This will give rise to new lines of research. Before discussing the further methodological implications of the proposed WEM in Chapter 7, however, in Chapter 6 I shall first look in more detail at how the diagonal of the WEM is filled in.

Completing the diagonal creates the theoretical and methodological space that is needed for an *ex ante* analysis of inequality. Systematic research on inequality and its various forms should play a greater role in standard analysis in economic research, both in terms of inequalities and differences between people, and between ecosystems and natural spaces. That is because economic science is not only concerned with *how much* wellbeing is created, but also with how it is *distributed* between people and nature, and *why*, and the prioritizations that people and institutions express about this when making choices. The local depletion of natural resources can lead to global problems. *Ex ante* distribution questions should also consider access to and the distribution of the shrinking 'eco-cake' amongst the growing world population in scenario studies. The very poorest often pay the highest price, and are more threatened by nature than the wealthy. I shall consider this further in Chapter 7 on sustainability. Finally, which value judgements and social justifications are made in relation to access- and distribution-related questions is important from both a political and an academic standpoint. After all, these value judgements and justifications are reflected in the prevailing economic theoretical arguments (discourse) and political programmes.

Table 2   The Wellbeing Economics Matrix (WEM): integration of WEM1, WEM2 & WEM3

from: Allocation of resources to:	Individuals (I)	Households (H)	Firms (F)	Social groups and communities (C)	Government (G)	Rest of the world (W)	Nature and space (N)	Net savings (NS)	Total Received
Individuals (I)	Allocation between individuals	Hi= Fi{Mh∩Rh∩Sh}	Fi= Fi{Mf∩Rf∩Sf}	Ci= Fi{Mc∩Rc∩Sc}	Gi= Fi{Mg∩Rg∩Sg}	Wi= Fi{Mw∩Rw∩Sg}	Nii= Fi{Mn∩Rn∩Sn}	NSi	U₁U₁{Hi;Fi;Ci;Gi; Wi;Ni;NSi}
Households (H)	Ih= Fh{Mi∩Ri∩Si}	Allocation between households	Fh= Fh{Mf∩Rf∩Sf}	Ch= Fh{Mc∩Rc∩Sf}	Gh= Fh{Mg∩Rg∩Sc}	Wh= Fh{Mw∩Rw∩Sw}	Nh= Fh{Mn∩Rn∩Sn}	NSh	U₁U₁{Ih;Fh;Ch;Gh; Wh;Nh;NSh}
Firms (F)	If= Ff{Mi∩Ri∩Si}	Hf= Ff{Mh∩Rh∩Sh}	Allocation between firms	Cf= Ff{Mc∩Rc∩Sc}	Gf= Ff{Mg∩Rg∩Sg}	Wf= Ff{Mw∩Rw∩Sw}	Nf= Ff{Mn∩Rn∩Sn}	NSf	U₁U₁{If;Hf;Cf;Gf; Wf;Nf;NSf}
Social groups and communities (C)	Ic= Fc{Mi∩Ri∩Si}	Hc= Fc{Mh∩Rh∩Sh}	Fc= Fc{Mf∩Rf∩Sf}	Allocation between social groups and communities	Gc= Fc{Mg∩Rg∩Sg}	Wc= Fc{Mw∩Rw∩Sw}	Nc= Fc{Mn∩Rn∩Sn}	NSc	U₁U₁{Ic;Hc;Fc; Gc;Wc;Nc;NSc}
Government (G)	Ig= Fg{Mi∩Ri∩Si}	Hg Fg{Mh∩Rh∩Sh}	Fg= Fg{Mf∩Rf∩Sf}	Cg= Fg{Mc∩Rc∩Sc}	Allocation between governments	Wg= Fg{Mw∩Rw∩Sw}	Ng= Fg{Mn∩Rn∩Sn}	NSg	U₁U₁{Ig;Hg;Fg;Cg; Wg;Ng;NSg}
Rest of the world (W)	Iw= Fw{Mi∩Ri∩Si}	Hw= Fw{Mh∩Rh∩Sh}	Fw= Fw{Mf∩Rf∩Sf}	Cw= Fw{Mc∩Rc∩Sc}	Gw= Fw{Mg∩Rg∩Sc}	Allocation between national economies	Nw= Fw{Mn∩Rn∩Sn}	NSw	U_wU_w{Iw;Hw;Fw;Cw; Gw;Nw;NSw}
Nature (N)	In= Fn{Mi∩Ri∩Si}	Hn= Fn{Mh∩Rh∩Sh}	Fn= Fn{Mf∩Rf∩Sf}	Cn= Fn{Mc∩Rc∩Sc}	Gn= Fn{Mg∩Rg∩Sg}	Wn= Fn{Mw∩Rw∩Sw}	Allocation between natural resources and spaces	NSn	U_nU_n{In;Hn;Fn;Cn; Gn;Wn;NSn}
Net investments (NI)	Nii	NIh	NIf	NIc	NIg	NIw	NIn	Balance between net savings and investments	NSi∩NSh∩NSf∩ NSc∩NSg∩NSw∩ NSn =NIi∩NIh∩ NIf∩NIc∩NIg∩ NIw∩NIn
Total provided	U₁U₁{Ih;If;Ic; Ig;Iw;In;NIi}	U₁U₁{Hi;Hf;Hc; Hg;Hw;Hn;NIh}	U₁U₁{Fi;Fh;Fc; Fg;Fw;Fn;NIf}	U₁U₁{Ci;Ch;Cf; Cg;Cw;Cn;NIc}	U₁U_g{Gi;Gh;Gf; Gc;Gw;Gn;Nig}	U₁U_w{Wi;Wh;Wf; Wc;Wg;Wn;Nlw}	U₁U_n{Ni;Nh;Nf; Nc;Ng;Nw;Nln}	U₁U_n{NSi;NSh;NSf; NSc;NSg;NSw;NSn}	**Collective Wellbeing**

6 Implications for methodology

When I studied economics at the University of Amsterdam in the 1990s, I had the good fortune to be taught by some extremely inspiring professors, including Mary Morgan, Guglielmo Carchedi, Susan Feiner and Deirdre McCloskey. They taught me qualitative knowledge and research skills, allowing me to reflect critically on the deconstruction of concepts and theoretical assumptions, the historical nature of economic ideas, and my own positionality as a budding economic researcher. Although I was equally interested in the design and calculation of econometric models, I would not have missed their classes for the world. They managed to inspire something in me that went beyond the world of numbers alone, and to express it in the right words. They kept pushing me to ask new questions, to take nothing for granted, to interrogate them about their own assumptions, and to be original and contrary, as long as there were well-founded reasons for this. That is why, in my opinion, economic methodology is not only about mastering quantitative methods and techniques, but equally about rudimentary excavations, deconstruction and reconstruction, linguistic skills, and creativity, originality and daring.

As today's economic students are usually trained to meet the demand for applied economic knowledge and skills in planning and policy, much economic education consists of methodological modules, in which both statistics and mathematics play a key role. At many economics faculties, economic education is mainly geared towards imparting quantitative knowledge and research skills. This has not always been the case, nor is it equally true of every faculty in the world. Perhaps this is a positivist or post-positivist trend that will soon have had its day. In this chapter, I argue that qualitative knowledge and research skills are also critically important in economics education. On the quantitative side, econometrics is a sub-discipline that has expanded over the last fifty years into a branch of economics that trains large numbers of future economists and financial analysts and planners. The specialized knowledge and skills that are needed to develop advanced models and then test them using empirical data are extremely important and useful, but not of interest to everyone. In today's economics education, the time that is dedicated to having students master the necessary skills and insights sometimes comes at the cost of courses on the history of ideas in economics, gender and ethnicity or political economy, for example – if these are offered at all. Based on a pluralistic vision of economics, I thus want to argue for a more balanced mix of research methods, quantitative and qualitative, in economics education.

In this chapter, I discuss several key methodological implications of 'Wellbeing Economics'. The list of implications is far from complete; it is merely a start, and a rather abstract one at that. I am therefore inviting others to put forward more detailed methodological considerations and applied analyses. The implications that I describe concern: (i) a place for post-positivism in economics; (ii) the combination of objective and subjective values; (iii) the analysis of intersections and interconnections in an inter-layered matrix; and (iv) the complex analysis of emergent and evolving properties. The development of new measures and indicators, a further step that clearly follows from this list of methodological implications, will be discussed separately in Chapter 7.

A place for post-positivism in economics

Over the past fifty years, economic research has been dominated by a positivist overtone that emphasizes quantitative approaches. Positivism assumes that scientific research must be based on systematic observations or measurements. Prior to this, economic science had been more heterodox, and classical economics had even been 'normative'. Keynes' economic analysis, for example, consisted of a mix of normative and logical reasoning and narratives (stories) about what a certain economic outcome should be (e.g., distribution of wealth or government policy). Keynesianism was an economic trend based on the ideas of Alfred Maynard Keynes (1883-1946), who promoted a mixed economy with an important role for the government alongside the private sector. It reached its heyday between 1945 and 1965. In 1976, the British economist Bob Coats described how 1965 had seen a paradigmatic break with the Keynesianism of the preceding years (p. 4). In the wake of this paradigmatic shift in the direction of positivism, economic science invested extensively in the development of increasingly advanced econometric models, and in gathering quantitative data to feed into these models. These could be used to make quantifiable predictions about the future. With ever-increasing precision, economists attempted to predict the future of the economy, so they could then search for quantifiable relations to explain the predicted changes.

At many economics faculties these days, the discipline of economics manifests itself almost as an exact science; as a natural science, as it were. According to the positivist scientific vision, knowledge about economic phenomena can only be gathered by undertaking systematic research into objectively observable, empirical and measurable data. That is why positivism is sometimes known as empiricism. Positivism also presumes that there is an independent relationship between the researcher and the subject. Top economics journals and expert institutes have contributed to this relative dominance of positivism in economics in recent decades.

It would be short-sighted to stereotype economics, however; we also find criticism of positivist dominance within the discipline. Many specialists in Marxist, feminist, political, anthropological and behavioural economics are critical of positivism. They embrace different, more subjective or constructivist scientific visions, which allow for the use of both qualitative and quantitative approaches. With the return of heterodox economics[35] as well

35 Ben Fine (2008) describes how, at the end of 1960, when he had just started studying economics, all of the leading economic journals paid much more attention to heterodox economics than they did 45 years later (p. 237).

as critical deconstruction from the outside, the core of economic science is slowly moving in a post-positivist direction. At the margins of the discipline, economics is much more heterodox. Post-positivism allows for both quantitative and qualitative approaches. The possibility of 'bias' is also recognized because the relationship between the researcher and their subject can never be considered fully independent. Furthermore, we are increasingly seeing an acknowledgement of 'context' in economic analysis and problem formulation, including in mainstream economic theories.

A brief reflection on the past and recent years, drawing on two examples of interesting economic studies (one from 1970 and one from 2014), shows that positivism has not always dominated leading economic research. In the following, I briefly describe two studies that are not dominated by the quantitative approach *per se*, but that are celebrated examples of economic studies that have made a substantial contribution to new insights and theory formation; one based on narrative analysis, the other on a historical analysis of economic statistics. For this reason, economics lecturers often cite these studies when teaching.

George Akerlof and information asymmetry

The first example is a study from 1970 by George Akerlof, who did research on information asymmetry in the second-hand car market. In the market for second-hand cars (popularly known as 'lemons' in the US), the seller knows more about the second-hand car than the buyer. This means that a situation of insecurity arises about the quality of the product for sale. As a consequence, car-buyers find it difficult to distinguish between good and bad second-hand cars, and they pay a price that lies somewhere in the middle. This results in a lower price for sellers of good second-hand cars, meaning that they leave the market. In the end, only sellers of bad second-hand cars remain in the market, and buyers pay a price for dishonesty as a result. Akerlof described this information asymmetry as the 'lemons problem'. His research is based almost entirely on logical reasoning and includes little data, the most important part of which consists of (qualitative) quotes. The article concludes with several normative observations about the role of institutions in solving information asymmetry problems (Akerlof 1970). Akerlof would later work with Michael Spence and Joseph Stiglitz, and the trio would win the Nobel Prize in Economics in 2001 for their analyses of market information asymmetries. Many economists have embraced this interesting insight into information asymmetry, and it is seen as an important critique of the 'rationality' assumption in neoclassical economics.

Thomas Piketty and growing inequality

The second example is a more recent important economic study, namely Thomas Piketty's book *Capital in the Twenty-First Century* (2014). This is based on a descriptive analysis of quantitative data. Piketty makes use of large, long-term datasets that allow him to carry out trend analyses. Using inductive reasoning,[36] Piketty derives a plausible explanation for and the economic relationship between income and assets, and formulates a hypothesis: namely, when capital grows faster than income, inequality increases. Piketty's recent study has already inspired many other studies and economic debates about the theme of 'inequality', and has led to new research questions.

Neither study features calculational models; evidently, such models are not a prerequisite for good economic analysis. What is more, in addition to objective data, both studies

36 In inductive research, a plausible conclusion is derived from bottom-up empirical research. This can lead to the formation of new theory. By contrast, deductive research tests an existing theory. We can also distinguish retroductive research, whereby a researcher reasons back from an observable concept to circumstances that led to this concept; and abductive research, which analyses data that initially fall outside an existing theory or framework.

leave room for subjectivity. After all, perceptions of quality influence the pricing of second-hand cars in Akerlof's thesis. Piketty, meanwhile, recognizes that the distribution of assets (although analysed objectively) will always have a subjective and psychological dimension within societies, because people simply have different opinions about what is just. Piketty is even normative in his recommendations, by proposing a global tax on assets in order to achieve a certain level of redistribution. Although Akerlof is not normative, he describes the value of market institutions that can resolve or reduce information asymmetries.

The 'Wellbeing Economics' perspective, which embraces pluralism, is thus critical of positivism due to the latter's emphasis on an exclusively quantitative approach and the assumption that there is a strict division between the researcher and the subject. Post-positivism seems to be a common factor in current initiatives and debates on 'Rethinking Economics'[37] and the 'Institute for New Economic Thinking'.[38] As post-positivism accepts that economic concepts, theories, methodologies and the background to research questions, for example, are always influenced by the researcher themselves, there can only be 'positional objectivity' at most. The researcher can use objective methods and techniques, but they always do this based on the particular position that is taken (Sen 1993). Thus, it is not possible to achieve complete objectivity in economic research; at most, we can refer to 'more objective' as compared to 'more subjective' research.

37 Rethinking Economics was founded in 2016 as an international network of critical economics students, academics and professionals calling for greater pluralism in economic science. In 2018, the network was active in nineteen countries around the world.

38 The Institute for New Economic Thinking (INET) was founded in 2007 with the aim of transforming economic debate and research with new, multi-disciplinary insights, and by embracing complexity and uncertainty in economic processes and acknowledging the role of history. It is thereby an attempt to break with 'traditional economics' (INET 2007: https://www.ineteconomics.org/about/our-purpose).

Room for alternatives

Through methodological and epistemological alternations and shifts such as these, economic science (like any science) remains subject to trends and trend-breaks. In addition to post-positivism, from a pluralistic perspective I also see increasing receptiveness to subjectivism (knowledge is strictly subjective – perception and conceptualization of reality by the subject) and critical realism (underlying mechanisms can explain observations and events) as epistemological starting points in economic research. In addition, the choice of a particular methodological approach or combination of approaches is also shaped by the formulation of the question, the research problem, and/or the context in which the research takes place. After all, the latter determines the relevance of the research, as well as the access to and interpretation of data. When the choice of methodology in economic research is dependent on the formulation of the question or problem, we also refer to a 'pragmatic' epistemological vision. Within pragmatism, practice is the most important touchstone of reality. For this reason, a pragmatic vision often forms the starting point for applied research, for example in the field of international development studies. In short, if we adopt a pluralistic perspective in economics, a number of epistemological approaches are possible. Post-positivism is currently becoming a characteristic trend in the field of economic science.

Objective and subjective values

Adopting a pluralistic vision also means taking an open approach to the selection of methods and techniques for data-gathering and analysis. The combination and/or integration of quantitative and qualitative methods and techniques is relevant from a 'Wellbeing Economics' perspective, because it allows us to combine objective and subjective values in research. After all, if we want to understand why people prioritize certain aspects of material or relational wellbeing, it is important to understand their subjective value judgements; and *vice versa*, we need to have a grasp of material wellbeing and relational wellbeing in order to understand how people assess their quality of life. As explained in Chapter 5, the WEM can be analysed in three ways: in terms of material, relational and subjective wellbeing. The three dimensions of wellbeing imply the use of different underlying scales and values. But how can objective data be analysed *in combination with* subjective data? And what role does narrative play? Objective data are measurable, whereas subjective data and narratives are not, because they are based on human experiences and opinions. Subjective wellbeing can partly be understood by using real data: people's experiences and perceptions. Real data are not directly observable (there are no observable data) and can only be known indirectly by ascribing a certain value to them, or known directly from stories and interpretations. The latter is known as narrative analysis. By using narrative analysis, objective and subjective data can be linked in a unique way by means of deductive, inductive and retroductive methods. But we do not need empirical data to carry out a narrative analysis; such analyses can also be based on abductive methods (see Chapter 1 for an explanation of these concepts).

In the discussion below, I focus on the combination of objective and subjective values, and thus on empirical analysis. In Figure 5 in Chapter 5, we saw that the three dimensions of the WEM are integrally linked. People constantly make complex trade-offs when making economic choices (i) between different dimensions of wellbeing, (ii) at different aggregation levels, and (iii) over time. That is because they can consider the different values (objective and subjective) simultaneously by looking at the *intersection* (or cross-section) of two or more sets: the point where everything converges. In mathematics, the symbol ∩ is used to indicate an intersection. At the intersection point, where an economic choice problem arises, several objective and subjective values can thus converge. For example, someone may earn a certain salary (*objective value 1*), do this in a particular work environment with colleagues (*objective/subjective value 2*),[39] and feel more or less satisfied with this (*subjective values 3 & 4*). With the aid of qualitative methods and techniques, such as narrative or descriptive analysis, we can look at mutual coherence between the values *1, 2, 3 & 4*. We can also investigate mutual coherence with the aid of quantitative methods and techniques, such as counting, ordering, prioritizing, correlation or an econometric model. If we also have data on multiple aggregation levels, such as individual income and family income (*objective values 1a & 1b*, possibly in combination with *objective/subjective value 2* and *subjective values 3 & 4*), we can make use of *nested models*. Nested models allow us to carry out multi-level analyses. Finally, if we have data over time, we can use all of these data to research time influences and do a trend analysis.

Economic choices are complex

Because wellbeing is multidimensional, and because both objective and subjective values are included in 'Wellbeing Economics', making economic choices is a complex problem. I shall explain what this means with reference to a simple example. In this choice problem, monetary and non-monetary values are weighed against one another, as well as values that represent different domains in which wellbeing is created (the paid and unpaid economies). Suppose that Mary, a single mother of three children, is looking for a new job. She currently works for the council, but she would like to switch to the private sector. She has a choice between two similar jobs; *job A*, which is close to home and pays better than her current job at the council, but less than she would earn in *job B*. In *job B* she would earn more, but it is further from home

39   The working environment can be measured with the aid of more objective data (e.g., number, education level, composition male/female etc.), as well as with more subjective data (social status of work environment, sustainability status, safety, etc.).

and would mean a longer commute. A comparison on the basis of competitive remuneration alone would lead to a simple trade-off between preferences in monetary terms (*Salary B* > *Salary A*, therefore she chooses *job B*). This entails trading off costs on one and the same underlying scale, namely a monetary scale with objectively measured units.

In view of Mary's family and care responsibilities at home, however, the daily commute will also play a role in her choice of job. A comparison in terms of travelling time alone would likewise result in a numerical trade-off, but now in terms of units of time (*Travelling time A* < *Travelling time B*, thus she chooses *job A*). This choice is different from the choice based on salary alone. Both comparisons, in terms of salary and travelling time, can be made separately in a more or less *objective* manner, but together they become a complex problem. After all, to what extent does a higher salary outweigh a longer commute? Mary's answer will be different from that of another individual. The trade-off between the values (time and money) in the two domains is therefore subjective. In practice, yet a third factor plays a role, namely that of career prospects. Mary wants to be promoted to a more senior role in the not-too-distant future. This will give her more satisfaction and economic independence. These are values that cannot be expressed in terms of time or money; they are purely subjective and lie in the personal sphere. But when realizing her career plans in the future, Mary can achieve different material values that are currently out of reach, in the form of a higher income and extra resources to get help with her caring responsibilities at home. This makes the trade-off between *job A* and *job B* even more complex. Moreover, the extent and nature of her caring duties will change in the future, meaning that her needs and priorities will change again. In practice, even more factors may play a role, such the desired business culture or atmosphere between colleagues. In this example, however, I limit myself to the three above. Mary's choice between *job A* and *job B* is thus composed of three different sets that converge at the point of choosing a job: 1) in monetary units, 2) in units of time, and 3) in terms of subjective perception. How does Mary ultimately make her choice? A composite choice can only be made when there is an implicit ranking order between each of these factors. In this example, there are *3!* permutations;[40] that is to say, *3x2x1=6* possible arrangements (see Table 3).

Table 3   Possible arrangements based on 3! permutations

Arrange- ment 1	Arrange- ment 2	Arrange- ment 3	Arrange- ment 4	Arrange- ment 5	Arrange- ment 6
Salary (B>A)	*Travelling time (A<B)*	*Career (A>B)*	*Career (A>B)*	*Salary (B>A)*	*Travelling time (A<B)*
Travelling time (A<B)	*Career (A>B)*	*Salary (B>A)*	*Travelling time (A<B)*	*Career (A>B)*	*Salary (B>A)*
Career (A>B)	*Salary (B>A)*	*Travelling time (A<B)*	*Salary (B>A)*	*Travelling time (A<B)*	*Career (A>B)*

Exactly how Mary makes this complex trade-off between *job A* and *job B* will depend on her needs and relative priorities. In principle, Mary can see more advantages in *job A* than in *job B*; after all, *A* dominates in terms of travelling time and career prospects, *B* only in terms of salary. If every factor is weighed equally in Mary's set, then she will choose *job A* on the basis of this trade-off. However, if the weight that she ascribes to salary is greater than that she ascribes to travelling time and career prospects together, she will still choose *job B*. Perhaps the extra earnings will allow her to meet her children's care needs, or to invest in extra training that will improve her career prospects in *job B* in the longer term. In this case, it is not possible to make an optimal choice, because the advantages of one job compared to the other do not all point in the same direction. The choice that Mary makes will thus be a sub-optimal choice; she will gain something in one or two dimensions, but give something up in another.

40   In mathematics, permutations show the number of possible arrangements of a set of observations (numbers, letters, other factors).

Figure 7　Two triangle diagrams for complex choices

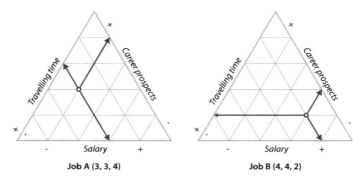

Job A (3, 3, 4)　　　　　　　　Job B (4, 4, 2)

A three-dimensional choice such as the one above can be re-presented mathematically in a triangle diagram. Mary wants to minimize her travelling time (-), but she wants to maximize her salary and career prospects (+). Figure 6 shows two such diagrams: on the left for *job A,* and on the right for *job B.*

Thus, in addition to income, Mary's everyday domestic situation, personal circumstances and career ambitions also play a role in her choice of job; and we have yet to even consider social conventions and (lack of) freedoms. Will her social surroundings allow her to make this choice by herself, or are there hard limits? Does she actually have a choice? Norms and freedoms, which are dependent on location and context, can play an important role in her eventual choice of job. To start with, when tackling this choice-problem we should ask whether Mary actually lives in a country and culture where she has the freedom to make her own choices.

The example above is one in which only three needs and priorities are considered, on the assumption that there is freedom of choice. In practice, even more factors can play a role. Moreover, these can change (rapidly) in context and over time with respect to one another, leading to different rankings over time. In short, making economic choices is a complex business. However, we need to recognize the complexity of economic choices in order to achieve more insight into the formation of economic theory on:
– the multi-dimensionality of needs and priorities;

- the mutability of these needs and priorities over time; and
- the influence of a socio-cultural and political context on freedom of choice and perceptions of what needs and priorities
  are.

Solving an economic problem can therefore involve making:
(i) Optimal choices – these are choices that lead to the fulfil-
    ment of needs and priorities in all selected dimensions of
    wellbeing. Suppose that, in the example above, the salary,
    travelling time and career prospects in *job B* were better in
    every respect than those in *job A;* in that case, choosing *job
    B* would clearly be the optimal choice for Mary.
(ii) Sub-optimal choices – these are choices that fulfil needs and
     priorities in one or more selected dimensions of wellbeing,
     but not in other dimensions. For example, Mary chooses a
     higher salary, but gives up spending time with her children
     in return. Sub-optimal choices are very common.
(iii) No choice – no choice is possible that leads to a positive
      change in the selected dimensions of wellbeing, because
      the opportunity, capacity or freedom is lacking to do this.
      This leads to an unavoidable deterioration of wellbeing in
      one or more of the selected dimensions.

Finally, I would like to add a fourth type of choice, inspired
by years of studying people and communities who attempt, in
deprived circumstances, to protect or improve their wellbeing.
These are choices that I would like to describe as 'contra-choices'.
Contra-choices are choices that are initially sub-optimal in all
selected dimensions of *current* wellbeing. Take, for example,
a small famer in Zambia who decides to migrate to the city in
search of work and a better future. He has no accommodation
there, and joins a group of informal hire-workers who live in a
slum on the edge of the city. Some days he finds work, other days
he does not. This also means that some days he has something
to eat, and other days he does not. As a result of this choice, he
surrenders his food security and accommodation, his family

relations (by leaving his family behind), and his mental stability and happiness. After some time, however, when this new urban migrant is able to exploit his abilities and opportunities to the full, one or more optimal choices may emerge. Whether this happens will depend on his stamina, among other things. From what I have seen and learned in situations of poverty, however, we should never underestimate human stamina; it sometimes seems inexhaustible. In the short term, this leads to making contra-choices, but the hope of a better future feeds human stamina to such an extent that an unknown outcome (things may turn out well or badly) is accepted. The fourth type of choice that we should distinguish is thus the contra-choice:

(iv) Contra-choices – ostensibly illogical but deliberate choices whereby human wellbeing deteriorates in all selected dimensions, and whereby the long-term outcome is unknown.

In summary, the Wellbeing Economics perspective distinguishes four types of choices that lead to known changes in some or all dimensions of the selected dimensions of wellbeing. With this step, we have bypassed the old dichotomy between so-called 'rational' and 'irrational' (or 'limited rationality') choices (see Table 4).

Table 4   Complex economic choices

Wellbeing	Δ *In all selected dimensions*	Δ *In some selected dimensions*
Positive	Optimal choice	Sub-optimal choice
Negative	Contra-choice	No choice

Analysing intersections and interconnectedness in an inter-layered matrix

In the previous section, the term *intersection* – the cross-section of two or more sets – was used several times. The use of intersections in economic analysis is an established methodology in choice theory. When this is done within the material dimensions of wellbeing alone, based on objectively measurable numbers, this is relatively simple. After all, the entities within the converging sets can all be measured in an objective way. With the aid of methodologies for calculating probability, the likelihood of an economic choice for a certain point where different dimensions converge (the intersection point) can be calculated for a group of economic agents, based on observed frequencies. When combining objective and subjective sets, the use of intersections is different, but not impossible. The following steps can be taken to systematically analyse intersections of multi-dimensional sets of functions. Objective and subjective values are expressed for one and the same *point observations* within one or more dimensions of wellbeing by using an econometric function; for example, quantitative and qualitative functions on 'income', such as amount (in money) and subjective sufficiency ('I earn too little, enough, more than enough'), or on 'travelling time', such as duration (in time units) and subjective perception (short, average, long).

(i)　An integrated *narrative* or *descriptive analysis* can be done, whereby the quantitative data is compared with the qualitative data in a substantively descriptive way.

(ii)　In doing so, we can make a distinction between *continuous data* (measurable data, e.g., income or time) and *discrete data* (a finite amount of whole numbers that can be counted or classified, e.g., in income categories per function).

(iii)　We can do a *process analysis, counting/percentages* and *ordinal analysis* of this by using *ratio/intervals*, and measure discrete data by means of *ordinal data* (ordering) or *nominal data* (only counting is possible).

(iv)　Measurement of *correlation* and *modelling analysis* of the underlying relations (e.g., between income level and subjective assessment, or between income level and function category).

(v)　*Complex modelling analysis* of *feedback mechanisms, timedependence,* or *tipping points* with the use of real, discrete and continuous data expressed in econometric functions.

Figure 8   Analysis of multi-dimensional intersections

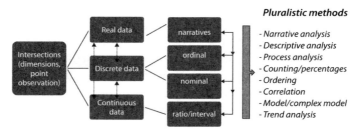

(vi) From a pluralistic perspective: all combinations of the methods above (i) together with (ii), (iii) and/or (iv) (see also Figure 8).

Figure 9 is a flattened, one-dimensional figure, just as the WEM (Table 2, Chapter 5) is a flattened, one-dimensional matrix. As explained in Figure 5 in Chapter 5, however, the WEM is inter-layered. One of the methodological implications of Wellbeing Economics is thus analysing the relationship between this inter-layered matrix and the System of National Accounts (SNA). In its current form, as it is set out in the UN guidelines, the SNA measures all of the economic processes within a country and a country's economic relations with other countries. In doing so, the following economic processes are identified: production, income generation, spending, income distribution and financing.

Figure 9   Analytical relations between the WEM and national accounts

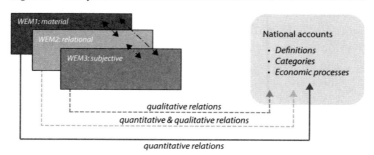

The SNA measures these economic processes using quantitative benchmarks.

Although for the time being, the WEM remains a theoretical idea in need of further methodological development, here I look ahead to the analytical opportunities presented by the three-dimensional WEM as input for economic policy-making and planning, based on its relations with the SNA. One important precondition for this relationship is that the same definitions and categories of economic agents and processes are used in the WEM and the SNA. These relations can be exclusively quantitative in nature, partly quantitative and partly qualitative, or wholly qualitative (see Figure 9). In short, there is a multitude of analytical methods and techniques available to the economist, of which econometric functions and models are just one method among many others.

Using the WEM1, which measures material exchange in the economy, quantifiable relations with the SNA are possible; using the WEM2, which looks at social relations and networks, quantitative and qualitative relations are possible; and using the WEM3, which measures subjective wellbeing alone, only qualitative relations are possible. Linking the WEM to the SNA is not possible for the time being, because, as explained in Chapter 5, the proposed WEM distinguishes two additional economic agents, individuals and social groups and communities, and nature is also included in the WEM framework. In Chapter 9, I shall describe several steps in more detail that are possible.

How to handle emergent and evolving properties

One oft-heard criticism of the discipline of economics is that economic models are drawn up on the basis of empirical observations from the past, so that predictions can be made about the future. These predictions often turn out to be incorrect. Moreover, these predictions are often 'point predictions', whereby the exact value of an economic outcome indicator (e.g., growth) is predicted. Such predictions tell us more about the form and parameters of the model used than about the analysis of underlying process factors, which are often viewed as a given. Critics see this failure to pay attention to analysing larger economic processes as a missed opportunity, leading to gaps in our knowledge about economic fluctuations and crises. After the international financial crisis of 2007-8, this criticism flared up again, but the problem is by no means new. As early as 1971, in his book on *The Political Economy of the New Left*, Assar Lindbeck published a list of objections to the then positivist turn in economics. These objections also resound in the current debate about 'Rethinking Economics':

(a) The failure to put sufficient emphasis on income distribution and explain this accordingly => *see current critique of the lack of attention paid to inequality in economic outcomes and processes.*

(b) The practice of viewing consumer preferences as a given, instead of as a subject for study and more detailed analysis => *see call for more attention to be paid to heterogeneity among economic agents.*

(c) The bias towards quantitative problems, and the disregarding of qualitative problems => *see call for multi-disciplinarity and pluralism.*

(d) The bias towards changes in the margin, at the expense of changes in the total system => *see emergence of complexity thinking in economics.*

(e) The failure to recognize the mutual relationship between economic and political processes, such as power structures and the historical context in which economic powers operate => *see call from institutional-historical economists.*

Source: Assar Lindbeck, 'The Political Economy of the New Left', p. 9; *my additions in italics*)

There is a similar call from the field of complexity thinking, now also emerging within economic science, for more attention to be paid to analysing underlying economic problems. Complexity thinkers prefer to talk in terms of 'economic systems', not 'economic processes', however; system thinking is simply more in line with the natural sciences, from which complexity theory originated. Despite this, complexity theory offers valuable insights about emergent and evolving economic properties. Emergent properties are properties that occur at a different economic organizational level; for example, by bringing together planks, stones, metal and glass and by using labour and machines to build a house, a residential function is created from the combination of all these factors. Evolving properties are properties that develop over time, such as medical knowledge and new insights about health. In complexity economics, the emphasis of the analysis lies on the interaction between individuals via networks in a (complex) economic system. Using various methods and techniques and with the aid of continuous and discrete data, it is then calculated which emergent/evolving and collective behaviour arises from a large number of heterogenous economic agents. Social and psychological behavioural factors and networks are included as possible explanations for this 'system behaviour'. Such analyses have given rise to new insights about economic change, feedback mechanisms, tipping points and the subjective aspects of these; for example, to explain a sudden change in the market, group behaviour when there is a crisis of confidence in banks, or the formation of political opinion on Europe. They also offer insight into sudden changes in the system by means of tipping points. However, the 'individual' in complexity theory has no definition or theory based on the social person. From a complexity economics perspective, people's social, cultural or political motivations to make certain trade-offs are difficult to place in an institutional framework. How power and powerlessness play a role in co-determining who has which choices, how free (or unfree) these choices are, and the historical background behind them, also fall beyond the horizon of contemporary complexity economics.

In Wellbeing Economics, however, an institutional and historical awareness is needed in order to gain more insight into economic processes and outcomes. Subjective factors, rooted in people's experiences and opinions, can help us to understand the underlying mechanisms. These underlying mechanisms can play an instrumental role in boosting or mitigating economic changes and trends, and at the same time they can explain a change at the margins that leads to a tipping point at a later point, or feedback in different economic processes.

If we fail to consider social and political institutions, we fail to take sufficient account of the complex trade-offs between monetary and non-monetary factors, and there is a high probability that certain subjective factors will remain completely out of the picture. These are then viewed as *exogenous* ('from the outside in') to the economic model. I am arguing, by contrast, that non-monetary factors, such as our relations with nature and subjectivities (e.g., power or trust), should be viewed as *endogenous* ('from the inside out') to an economic model. Within an economic model, for example, these non-monetary factors can be included as absolute marginal values (minimum or maximum). In Chapter 1, 'Change the Goal', of her book *Doughnut Economics*, Kate Raworth (2017) sets out proposals regarding the ecological limits that would allow the economy to function sustainably (following Johan Rockström's basic ideas about the nine planetary boundaries, 2009). Social limits can be identified and calculated in the same way (marginal value of poverty or inequality, basic access to education and health, and so forth). In addition, non-monetary factors can be included in the form of a precondition in an economic model, for example, by making individual prioritizations of resources dependent on the prioritizations of others (within a household or social group/community). This gives rise to an emergent socio-economic model that takes account of complex social relations and the influence of networks. Finally, qualitative data can be translated numerically in an economic model or indicator, for example by weighting a fall in income for the very poorest more heavily than a fall for the very richest, or by building in a different weighting or leverage factor as a numerical translation of qualitative data (for example, of a social category), following the justice-based ideology of John Rawls (1971).[41] In this way, qualitative and quantitative data can be integrated into economic methodology in an innovative way, producing better-informed economic models and scenario calculations. These methodological innovations are sorely needed if we want to be able fully to analyse and manage today's economic problems of increasing inequality and unsustainability. I focus on these two themes in the following chapters: Chapter 7 on 'A Focus on Inequality' and Chapter 8 on 'A Sustainable Economy'.

41 In *A Theory of Justice* (1971), John Rawls advances two basic principles that lie at the heart of his theory of justice. According to the first principle, everyone has an equal right to a total system of equal basic freedoms, consistent with an equivalent system of freedom for all. According to the second principle, social and economic inequalities between people and groups of people should most benefit the person or group who is worst off, as well as be linked to functions and relations that are accessible to all, under the condition of fair equality of opportunity.

7   A focus on inequality

When Thomas Piketty published his book *Capital in the Twenty-First Century* in 2014, his call for a greater focus on inequality was well-timed. Never before had the gap between rich and poor grown so rapidly. When we discuss inequality in economics, it is important to make a distinction between two forms of inequality: income inequality and wealth inequality. Income inequality usually relates to the income that people earn by means of work; this can be formal or informal labour (g). By wealth, we mean the financial and other material and non-material property (shares, homes, durable assets) from which the owner indirectly earns an income, in the form of interest, rents or speculative gains (r). Income inequality and wealth inequality are linked: the more income someone earns, the more income can be transformed into wealth. Piketty (2014) shows that in the past fifty years, wealth in rich Western and emerging economics rose faster than wealth. Trade unions and social partners have lost voice, and this is reflected in lower or no wage increases. By contrast, returns on income from capital have grown more rapidly ($r>g$). This difference in growth has led to an increase in inequality between the 'haves' and the 'have-nots'. At the end of the book, Piketty therefore argues that income from capital should be taxed more heavily around the world, in order to redistribute part of this continuing asset growth from the wealthy to the less fortunate.

The 2020 World Economic Forum (WEF) report recognizes that increasing inequality and polarization threaten the stability, cohesion and further growth of the global economy, but sees no reason for structural political-economic reforms. The WEF only proposes changes within the framework of the neoliberal model, in the form of mobilization, cooperation and innovation in the direction of sustainability in the private sector. It does not discuss what might encourage the private sector to embrace sustainability, or how this would lead to less inequality. The increase in inequality over the last four decades, as described by

Piketty, was followed by Brexit and the election of Donald Trump as President of the United States in 2017. These days, criticism is a core element of the meetings surrounding the WEF in Davos, Switzerland. Critics not only argue against increasing inequality, but also against the neoliberal capitalist political-economic model, on the grounds that it promotes inequality. According to the critics, 'free market forces' strengthen rather than weaken existing inequalities, because the power to steer market forces lies in the hands of the 'happy few'. As a result, 'sustainability' and 'charity' are reserved for those who can afford them, but are too expensive for low-income groups. By 2017, the neoliberal economic model had revealed a continuous tendency towards polarization. A more socially responsible, sustainable model, with a regulating and distributing government that takes responsibility for nature, and in which citizen participation is guaranteed, is needed to prevent or manage this ongoing tendency towards economic polarization.

In the rest of this chapter, I shall discuss how inequality can be made an *a priori* part of economic analysis, so that it can be addressed in policy planning. This will allow distribution issues to play a more prominent role in the discipline of economics, as well as the standard analysis and prediction models of economic growth and production.

Growing inequality

As with Piketty's (2014) book, in Branko Milanovic's book entitled *Global Inequality* (2016) it is shown empirically how inequality has increased in high-income countries (e.g., in Europe, America, Oceania) and emerging economies (e.g., China, India, Thailand, Indonesia, Vietnam) over the past 25 years. Such a rise in inequality in high-income countries is at odds with the traditional Kuznets curve (see Figure 6). This is because the Kuznets curve, based on the ideas of the Nobel Prize winner Simon Kuznets (1901-1985), predicted that inequality is low when a country has a low income level, increases when its economy grows, and falls again when a high level of income is reached. This led to the formulation of the Kuznets curve as an inverted U-curve. At present, we are not seeing the expected continuing fall in inequality with a high level of income in middle- and high-income countries. Instead, we are seeing increasing inequality; for example, in the United States, the United Kingdom, Germany and Sweden. For the period 1998-2008, real income growth was highest for people around the 50% point of global income distribution (the median) *and* for the wealthiest 1%. The majority of the wealthiest 1% are to be found in high-income countries (North America, Western Europe, Japan, Oceania). Real income growth was lowest for people around the 80% point of global income distribution, most of whom belong to the lower middle classes in high-income countries (Milanovic 2017: p. 11). These differences ensured growing income inequality in high-income countries. Branko Milanovic concludes from this that the effects of globalization are ambivalent (p. 30): some benefit, others do not. According to Milanovic, this change is never unequivocal.

Although the Kuznets curve was originally drawn up on the basis of cross-sectional data from a series of countries, the curve was also used to characterize the course of inequality *within* countries. In Branko Milanovic's book, however, this inverted U-curve is more like an upside-down S-curve, whereby almost zero-point growth is observed around the 80% point of global income distribution. Based on the comparative empirical data analysis that Branko Milanovic carried out for 120 countries, we see that over the long term, it is more a case of wave-like fluctuations in inequality; inequality within countries repeatedly rises and falls (see Figure 10).

According to Branko Milanovic, these fluctuations are due more to changing national political-economic climates, combined with the effects of globalization, than to increased prosperity. This gives economists an alternative line of approach for analysing inequality, one that is linked to social and political

Figure 10   The Kuznets curve and fluctuations in inequality

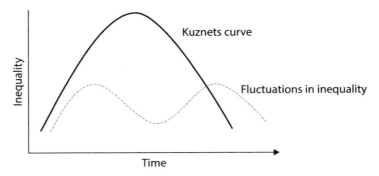

institutions, historical choices and changes in policy, as well as what is happening in the rest of the world; because China exports cheap products to the United States, for example. Inequality is thus embedded in social and political processes and cannot be viewed in isolation from them, as we saw in Figure 3, Chapter 4 of this book. Based on his long-term analysis, Milanovic observes that inequality in the United Kingdom and United States in the period 1850-1950 followed the inverted U-form of the Kuznets curve almost exactly (Milanovic, 2017: p. 44). After 1980, however, the trend in inequality no longer followed the curve; instead, inequality rose again. Piketty (2014) attributes this rise in inequality in high-income countries to the neoliberal political-economic model; due to the great differences in income and (especially) assets, the wealthy manage to benefit more from globalization than the non-wealthy. They generate income from capital, can invest their wealth (internationally), seek out tax advantages, and profit from financial expertise. However, Piketty's statement implies that inequality should invariably rise with capitalist development – and that has not always been the case. If we look at the period before the beginning of the twentieth century, inequality did in fact fall with capitalist development. Milanovic's long-term analysis shows that periods of rising and falling inequality alternate, whilst the average income level rises. The correlation between income, growth and inequality is by no means straightforward. At the end of his second chapter, Milanovic therefore concludes that from a historical perspective, there does not seem to have been a trade-off between more growth or more equality – even though this is what the dominant discourse would have us believe, and it is what political parties are keen to underline. Milanovic's long-term empirical analysis shows that this is a misconception.

Inequality as an important economic measure

The theme of inequality thus plays a major role in recent books by Thomas Piketty (2014) and Branko Milanovic (2017). As a measure of how well or badly an economy is doing, however, 'inequality' hardly has the same status as the economic growth indicator. National economic policy is more focused on growth than on equality or sustainability; the latter are seen largely as social policy. Moreover, for many political parties, 'social policy' issues in general, and redistribution in particular, can only be raised once the precondition of economic growth has been met. When the economy stagnates or shrinks, as is currently the case in 2020, the issue of redistribution is swiftly removed from the political agenda. This also applies to questions of sustainability. The Netherlands is lagging behind other countries in the world (e.g., Germany, Norway, etc.) with respect to investing in a sustainable economy, for example; the investments that are being made are being financed primarily from economic growth, and less from taxation.

The value that is attached to the economic growth indicator is many times greater than the value attached to equal distribution, despite the fact that (in)equality is an important indicator of the state of inter-human relations in an economy. Social cohesion, solidarity, trust and public spirit also serve an economic purpose. If these are lacking, investments and contracts are more likely to be seen as risky, because there is no mutual trust, and there is the threat of social and political conflict (e.g., in Nigeria, South Africa and Brazil). Extreme inequality also brings the problem of structural exclusion and conflict between the 'haves' and the 'have nots', which can seriously damage social, political and economic stability and sustainability, and lead to the undermining of future growth due to under-investment, conflict, disasters and other economic shocks. The focus on economic growth is politically determined; the degree to which inequality is also considered differs along whole political spectrum.

There is also an epistemological factor at the heart of this, however: if economic theories continue one-sidedly to emphasize material welfare and individualism, the dominance of the economic growth indicator is hardly surprising. After all, according to the 'methodological individualism' assumption explained in Chapter 3, the welfare of every individual will increase if the average total welfare in an economy increases. It is argued that everyone benefits from growth and free trade, thanks to 'trickle-down' effects. Within the framework of neoclassical economic theory, there is no space, conceptually or functionally, to problematize *a priori* the relationship with distribution and sustainability. There are simply no points of departure for this in the current economic growth model.

Structural inequalities in society lead to economic blockages, a tendency towards monopolization, instability, misallocation and dissatisfaction. These hinder 'trickle-down' effects, meaning that not everyone automatically benefits from economic growth. For example, the sociologist and historian Charles Tilly has written about how deeply-rooted structural inequalities are perpetuated for generations, because inequalities affecting certain groups of people (e.g., women, minorities) are reproduced by social, political and economic institutions and embedded in unequal power relations (Tilly 1998). It is therefore important to think about supplementary economic indicators and measures of economic progress, in order to reflect the economic reality of the *entire* population accurately from a wellbeing perspective. I shall consider this in more detail in Chapter 9.

From a Wellbeing Economics perspective, the focus on inequality and sustainability is self-evident, because it reflects the relational dimension of wellbeing, as well as people's subjective assessments of their economic allocation. This brings economic issues of 'distribution', 'sustainability' and 'justice' back to the core of economic research – which is where they belong, in my opinion. The question of 'Who gets what and why?' thereby becomes at least as important as 'How much do I get?' The nature-relational dimension implies that sustainability and the quality of growth are always taken into account, and the socio-relational dimension implies that internal differences are included in the economic analysis. Inequality can affect the functioning of the economy at both an individual and a collective (aggregated) level. Too much inequality can lead to dissatisfaction and conflict; too little, by contrast, can put a check on self-initiative, competition and innovation. It is not easy to achieve a balance. The right balance is associated with broad societal visions and sentiments regarding inequality and social justice, and is itself subject to change. How much and what people are prepared to share with others and nature, and under what conditions, differ according to time and place, as shown by the great differences in social security systems, taxation, and the size and quality of public provisions between countries and sections of the population. In addition, major differences of opinion can arise over what is perceived as a 'just' distribution. According to the subjective perception of wellbeing, there will be different priorities within economies with regard to inequality and growth. More equality does not mean less growth *per se*, although the political debate often assumes this to be the case.

Analysing inequality in the WEM

As a general rule, the diagonals of social accounting matrices (SAMs) are not filled in. This makes little sense, because it is precisely on the diagonal that inequality *between* economic agents can be problematized. It would in theory be possible to fill in the diagonal on a traditional SAM, even though inequality would then be measured in a single monetary dimension alone. This is not standardly done, however, because it would first be necessary to take decisions about which categories of economic agents should be used to map out inequality. As a result, such analysis is done *post facto*. Not every government wants to reveal the inequalities that exist between ethnic groups, religious groups, or men and women; there is a fear of generating social unrest. This is where political choices come up against economic issues. As explained in Chapter 5, the traditional SAM is one-dimensional: all flows of goods and services between economic agents are expressed in a single value, money. Within this monistic framework, inequality is also expressed in terms of money alone; mostly income/expenditure or assets, using the Gini coefficient, for example.[42] But inequality can also be expressed in numerous other variables, such as years of education, health indicators, amount of durable property, number of social networks, hours of leisure time, and so forth. In principle, every ratio/interval, nominal or ordinal variable could be used to express an economic inequality (see also Figure 8, Chapter 6). We can also use the theoretical framework of the three-dimensional WEM (Table 2 & Figure 9, Chapter 5) to express the subjective dimensions of inequality, for example by asking people about their 'perceptions' of inequality. How satisfied/dissatisfied are people with their quality of life, for example, and what do they consider to be important aspects of collective wellbeing, for which they would be prepared to give up something in return? This is very important, because these perceptions can differ by country and culture. In this way, the complex relationship between, for example, income inequality, what people perceive to be 'equal' or 'unequal', and the extent to which people are prepared to tackle this collectively, is investigated from multiple

42   The Gini coefficient is a statistical measure that is used in economics to measure inequality in the distribution of income or assets.

perspectives. By filling in the diagonal of the WEM, we can consider *a priori* multi-dimensional inequalities between individuals, households, firms, social groups and communities, businesses and governments, as well as the subjective values that are attributed to them and the distributive systems that flow from them (I look further at the idea of the 'distributive economy', developed by Kate Raworth among others, in Chapter 8). By considering social relations and networks, too, we can do a more penetrating analysis of the equality of opportunity and how best to capture this in our economic model. Based on the WEM (Table 2) and Figure 4 on the different allocation mechanisms in the economy, Table 5 identifies the various ways to assess social equality. These consist of economic agents, processes and allocation mechanisms that can function as starting points for a systematic analysis. Column 3 of Table 5 shows the dominant allocation mechanisms. These do not exclude other forms of allocation, however; for example, a social enterprise can also contribute to reciprocity and support in local communities, or to distribution through a social programme for employees. The same applies to all other economic agents. The 'rest of the world' can allocate goods and services through market exchange, but it can also support other countries and population groups with international aid programmes, or contribute to redistribution (e.g., when a natural disaster strikes).

Table 5   Assessing social equality: agents, processes and mechanisms

Economic agent	Processes	Dominant mechanisms
Individuals		All mechanisms
Households		Reciprocity and support; redistribution
Firms and businesses	– Consumption	Market exchange
Social groups and communities	– Production – Redistribution	Reciprocity and support
Governments	– Co-creation	Redistribution
Rest of the world		Market exchange
Hybrid partnerships		All mechanisms

Associative thinking

Studying such complex relationships between objective and subjective values and economic behaviour requires considerable associative thinking skills. Whereas linear thinking is important for logically distinguishing cause and effect – for example, someone is underprivileged because they are illiterate – it is often limited to the material dimension; the link between cause and effect is expressed in terms of indicators that can be measured objectively. In this case, the underlying problem is attributed exclusively to a singular unit of observation; an individual's education, in this particular example. As a consequence, the responsibility of the underlying cause of 'being underprivileged' is also attributed to this singular unit of observation, namely, someone's lack of schooling. The solution is subsequently sought in universal access to education. This may not solve the underlying problem *per se*, however, and this is something we often see in practice. A number of factors may play a role in someone being economically 'underprivileged'; the causes may lie in the social domain (e.g., social standards) or in the political domain (e.g., caste inequality). Unless we address these other factors, this 'underprivileged individual' will be unable to complete their education or succeed in finding work. When the same problem is tackled in a more associative way, the relationships between the different factors can be identified more quickly. Something that often plays a role in problems such as 'inequality' is intersectionality: the idea, in sociology and certain political debates, that individuals/groups in a society experience structural discrimination and oppression based on multiple factors. These inequality factors have the tendency to overlap and negatively reinforce one another. From a linear perspective, intersectionality is difficult to penetrate. Unravelling intersectionality requires powers of observation and the ability to think associatively. My argument is thus that in order to gain more insight into economic inequality and the economic choices that are made in relation to this by individuals and societies, associative thinking is at least as important as, if not more so than, linear thinking.

It is partly for this reason that I have always recognized the added value of the multi-disciplinary approach in economic science, as new associations can be discovered and new questions can arise from the dialogue and disagreement between different disciplines. That is not to say that I see no space for linear thinking in economics. On the contrary; I see space for both linear and associative ways of thinking, mono- and multi-disciplinary approaches, methods and techniques. Our selection depends on the economic problem at hand. In the case of a complex phenomenon such as 'inequality', there is currently a great need for multi-disciplinary approaches. In recent decades, economic science has tended to develop in accordance with the trend towards mono-disciplinarity. If an exclusively linear perspective is taken, however, economists are unable to give a complete explanation for inequality and its underlying causes. The most fruitful approach to unravelling the complexity of inequality is to alternate between a more associative approach and linear methods that help to provide an insight into trends and shifts.

There is increasing pressure from heterodox movements in economics to return to greater pluralism in economic science. In 2015, 65 student associations from 30 countries wrote an open letter calling for more pluralism in economics books and education.[43] I am also aware, though, of the political motives for paying insufficient attention to a topic such as economic inequality and inclusivity. If there were a greater political focus on inequality, there would be more demand for inequality analyses in economics and the associated measures (see also: Pouw and Gupta 2015). With a growing global population and shrinking ecological space and natural resources, new inequalities will emerge, and will increasingly concern access to and control over natural resources and natural space. This is all the more reason

43   See International Student Initiative for Pluralism in Economics (2014-2015) *Open Letter*, http://www.isipe.net/open-letter/

for economists to try to gain more insight into the relationship between inequality, wellbeing and sustainability. Associative thinking should be developed and stimulated more effectively as part of economics education, in addition to linear thinking based on established structures, categories and discrete units.

8   A sustainable economy

While on a research trip to Busia and Kisumu in Western Kenya in 2012, accompanied by some students from the University of Amsterdam, I noticed that almost all of the trees had disappeared from the small villages surrounding Lake Victoria. A rich biodiversity of tree species grow in the area's humid tropical ecosystem. Most of the trees had disappeared, however, because they had been felled for wood production or used by the inhabitants themselves for fuel. Due to rapid population growth, the intensification of (small-scale) agriculture and regular flooding along the lake and rivers, land in Busia had become scarce. Space for trees and forest was sacrificed for human development and more agriculture. A local clan leader told me that people missed the trees, because they had also provided shade, borne fresh fruit (mango, avocado, jack fruit), helped with rainwater retention, and prevented land erosion. We know from climatological research that trees and forests also have an important influence on the atmosphere. The timing of the two annual rainy seasons had shifted and they had become shorter, leading to longer periods of drought. To the frustration of the clan leader, however, no one had taken the initiative to plant new trees. The clan leader had now found a girls' secondary school that was willing to cultivate tree seedlings and sell them at cost price to village residents in the school's public grounds. In this way, the clan leader hoped to see the trees return to the homes and farms and the wider surroundings. It is in the interests of both humans and nature to protect and restore natural resources. Lying at the core of the concept of 'sustainability' is the idea of conserving something over time. In the case of nature, this means preserving natural resources for future generations. In this book, sustainability is defined in relation to economics as *'economic development coupled with a reduction of environmental pressure on nature'*. Thus, sustainability is primarily about the *quality* of economic processes, not about quantity or economic growth. More growth is not always better. At present, however, the global economy is still on a path to unsustainable growth. Economic contraction is not the answer, because economic activities can also be polluting and unsustainable during economic contraction or 'degrowth'. Although aviation and road traffic fell silent during the COVID-19 crisis, and there was a sharp rise in air and water quality across the world, this was achieved at the expense of employment, and many people lost their jobs. In essence, this is about *the quality of economic growth*. We need to reassess the conditions of this growth from the perspective of nature and human beings; that is to say, under which circumstances and with what means are natural resources and space used in economic processes (production, consumption, redistribution and co-creation), and what short- and long-term consequences does this have for nature in general, and for our eco-systems and wellbeing in particular? In theory, it must be possible to achieve sustainable growth by de-coupling economic growth from environmental pollution and the depletion of natural resources and space. Thus, a sustainable economy does not mean an economy where no growth can or may take place *per se*. A sustainable economy puts the emphasis on the quality (not quantity) of growth, and on preserving natural resources.

Nine planetary boundaries

Since the publication of the Club of Rome's *Limits to Growth* report in 1971, sustainability has become a key theme in economics. For the first time, people became aware on a large scale of the finite nature of the current process of economic growth, on a finite planet. With an ever-growing global population that is using more and more raw materials, emitting increasing amounts of CO_2 and putting more and more pressure on natural resources, green space and landscapes (the shrinking 'eco-cake'), sustainability has become more urgent than ever before. Only now does this awareness seem to be leading to significant behavioural changes in economic practice, through the transformation of production, consumption, distribution and co-creation processes. The question is whether there is still time to turn the economic tide.

In 1987, the Brundtland Commission built on the ideas from *The Limits to Growth*, defining sustainable development as 'development that meets the needs of the present without compromising the ability of future generations to meet their own needs' (Source: Brundtland Report, p. 15). The idea that there are limits to the process of economic growth has developed into the current notion of 'planetary boundaries'; the idea that humanity can only function safely within the limits of the Earth and its ecosystems, in order to preserve them for the future. Johan Rockström and his team at the Stockholm Resilience Centre identified nine ecological terrestrial and marine processes that together determine life on Earth. These sociological processes are captured in dynamic ecosystem models that can calculate the interaction between the physical surroundings and their biological functions over time and space. Based on ecosystem models such as these, the team calculated nine planetary boundaries, four of which have already been significantly exceeded to date (see Table 6). But what precisely will this crossing of ecological boundaries (thresholds) mean in the longer term? Are these processes really irreversible? And how do the nine processes influence one other? Are there tipping points that lead to an acceleration of negative trends? These are all questions that are currently being investigated by interdisciplinary teams of scientists. It is likely that there are yet more processes to identify, in addition to the nine ecological processes; the approach does not claim to be comprehensive or perfect. The nine planetary boundaries offer a framework for thinking and calculation, in order to monitor these carefully in conjunction with the functioning of the economy and the type of growth path that is followed.

The recycling economy and the circular economy

In current thinking and debates about the transition to a more sustainable economy, increasing attention is being paid to the

Table 6   The nine planetary boundaries

Planetary boundary	Indicator	Boundary	Today
1. Climate change	CO_2 in atmosphere	350	400
2. Loss of biodiversity	Number of species that go extinct each year, per million	10	>100
3a. Nitrogen cycle	– Amount of N_2 extracted from the atmosphere by humans each year	35	121
3b. Phosphorus cycle		11	9
	– Amount of P that ends up in the oceans each year		
4. Atmospheric ozone	Concentration of ozone	276	283
5. Acidification of oceans	Average saturation level of aragonite in ocean water	2.75	2.90
6. Global fresh water consumption	Fresh water consumption per person	4,000	2,600
7. Land use	Amount of land used for agriculture	15	11.7
8. Chemical pollution	Concentration of toxic materials, plastics, endocrine disrupters, heavy metals and radioactive waste in the environment	Unknown	Unknown
9. Aerosols in the atmosphere	Concentration of particles in the atmosphere	Unknown	Unknown

Significant exceedance is shown in grey.
Source: Rockström et al. 2009

concept of the circular economy. The term 'circular economy' is used to describe an economy in which raw materials are repeatedly re-used and waste is minimized, or would ideally disappear altogether. The circular economy is related to the recycling economy ('re-use economy'), but it goes further. In the circular economy, the aim is to produce and consume without any leftover waste. The recycling economy aims to re-use products as much as possible, but waste is still left over from production and consumption processes. The difference between the recycling economy and the circular economy is visualized in Figure 11.

Figure 11   The recycling economy and the circular economy

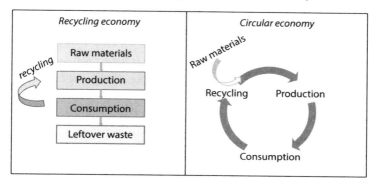

Source: adapted from Rijksoverheid Nederland 2019

In principle, the circular economy goes further than the recycling economy, because producers take account of the potential for the re-use (or total consumption) of the product to be manufactured. Re-use is already considered at the design stage, for example, by manufacturing with recyclable glass, paper and cardboard. The Dutch government aims to have a circular economy by 2050, which means that the economy will run entirely on recyclable raw materials. Various measures and agreements are being concluded for this purpose with the commercial sector. The following five business sectors in the Dutch economy should be the first to go circular: biomass and the food industry, synthetic materials, manu-facturing industry, construction and consumer goods. Consumer behaviour is also influenced by waste reduction programmes and environmental awareness programmes, for example. With the 'Plastic Pact', the government and the commercial sector are working together to produce less plastic waste and to make leftover waste re-usable. When new buildings are built and property renovated, central government has also set the target of using as many recyclable and raw materials as possible. After 2018, all new buildings must be energy-neutral. All of these developments form part of the effort to achieve a sustainable economy, in which nature conservation is still seen as going hand-in-hand with economic growth. The question, however, is whether the two are compatible. How can we recycle energy consumption, for example, and what if more raw materials go into a production process than come out? Raw materials are being depleted. New technological products contain many raw materials that have been assembled in a complex way, and it may be difficult to separate them again. What should be done with this leftover technological waste? It is by no means certain that this will prevent the depletion of natural resources, but this is a matter that is worth pursuing.

Critics are doubtful whether the circular economy will be the solution as long as we continue to pursue economic growth. Ideas about degrowth are therefore being explored, for example by the political ecologist Giacomo D'Alisa and colleagues (2017). Rather than making the case for economic contraction (like a standard opponent of economic growth) in his work on degrowth, he argues for 'flourishing', whereby human development is driven by a wide range of values other than maximizing consumption and money. The values associated with flourishing include autonomy, solidarity, happiness and wellbeing. Multiple new citizen initiatives, based on these values and grouped under the term 'new/creative commons', are being undertaken to achieve societal objectives. In these initiatives, cooperation and sharing are more important than realizing economic growth. The worldwide degrowth movement mainly focuses on economic practice, which is a pragmatic starting point. The movement is still seeking a coherent theoretical framework or unambiguous epistemological perspective to provide the basis for economic theory formation and policy analysis. Although I embrace the idea of 'flourishing' instead of 'growth', I do not think that a sustainable economy need rule out growth; rather, growth should simply not be the (only) compass used to steer the economy.

The doughnut economy

As argued in Chapter 5 with reference to Figure 6, humans have an ambivalent relationship with nature. We are dependent on natural resources for our survival on Earth, but under certain circumstances nature also poses a threat to humans (natural disasters, dehydration, wild animals, viruses). Humans have a collective duty to preserve the natural world, but the objective of a sustainable economy goes further than nature conservation. When it comes to the economy, nature is both instrumentally and intrinsically valuable. On the one hand, natural resources and space form input for economic production processes, and it is important that they do not become depleted. On the other hand, natural resources, landscapes, seas, rivers, mountains and green spaces have intrinsic significance for the quality of life on Earth. If all green space and landscapes were to disappear, levels of human wellbeing would plummet.

Building on the work of Johan Rockström and his team, in 2012 the British economist Kate Raworth introduced the idea of the 'doughnut economy'. Her later book, *Doughnut Economics* (2017), is based on the idea of a distributive and regenerative economy. By this, she means that social and ecological processes are linked to certain minimal limits in order to guarantee the human wellbeing of everyone on Earth. Distribution and ecological regeneration are of vital importance to a healthy economy in the long term. This requires an economy that is both resilient and adaptable; after all, social and ecological processes are also subject to complex dynamics (within set limits). The economy needs to be able to respond to these in good time.

The social limits form the inner edge of the doughnut, and together represent the 'social foundation' on which every society should rest. The ecological limits form the outer edge, and together represent the 'ecological ceiling' (see Figure 12). The doughnut crust itself represents the (ecological) safe and just space in which humankind can operate. According to Raworth's doughnut compass, every economic process that results in people falling below the social minimum, or in our irretrievably overshooting a planetary limit, should be redesigned.

How to get there, and who should be responsible for what in this process of rethinking and redesigning, remains a political

Figure 12   The doughnut economy

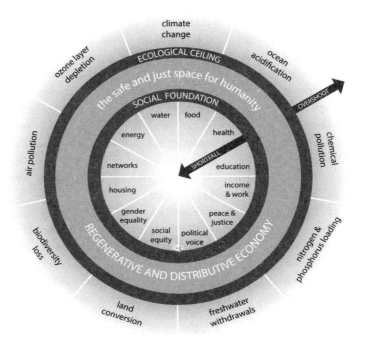

Source: Raworth 2017

issue. The process is complicated by power and resources, short-term profits and one-sided interests. As economists, we therefore cannot avoid undertaking far-reaching political and economic analyses in order to achieve a better understanding of the risks, obstacles and breaking points in the transformation to a sustainable economy. Although the use of political-economic analysis as a method falls beyond the scope of this book, I nevertheless want to emphasize its importance here, because it helps us to map out the power relations that determine economic processes and outcomes. The WEM (Table 2, Chapter 5) can help to guide and give substance to this type of economic analysis at different scale levels. Kate Raworth links the debate about sustainability directly to social issues, distinguishing the following twelve social processes: (i) nutrition, (ii) health, (iii) education, (iv) income and work, (v) peace and justice, (vi) political voice, (vii) social equality, (viii) gender equality, (ix) housing, (x) networks, (xi) energy, and (xii) water. Each of these social processes can be measured using selected indicators. Raworth employs existing indicators for this, but we could also use alternative measures (see Chapter 9) that represent context- and time-specific social circumstances. Raworth's point is that when a society is unable safely to provide this minimal social foundation for all, this society will fall short and fall into the 'hole' of the doughnut, as it were. Her table of measured social indicators was drawn up in 2012; seven years on, we can see that much is still to be gained from them at a global level (see Table 7). The indicators are illustrative, and partly chosen on the basis of the available data. 'Peace and security' and 'networks' are not included in the table below, although they are named in the doughnut (Figure 12). In their place, 'resilience' is measured using the multi-dimensional poverty indicator. The visualization with the aid of the doughnut suggests that Raworth perceives links between social (in)equality and sustainability, but she does not explain precisely how these relationships work. Indeed, the relationship between social (in)equality and sustainability is by no means straightforward. In primitive societies, 'sustainability' is often embedded in a way of life (e.g., that of nomad tribes or small fishing communities), whilst in high-income countries, it is currently said that 'sustainability' is a choice reserved for the 'happy few', the 'eco-class'. These are two different debates, as it were, showing how the relationship between social (in) equality and sustainability is always context- and time-specific. The fact is that high-income countries put more pressure on the environment than low-income countries. But there are major differences in social equality between high-income countries, and the same is true of low-income countries.

Whereas the social limits above indicate the social foundation, Rockström's nine planetary boundaries represent the ecological ceiling. When a society overshoots this ceiling, we undermine

Table 7   Global deprivation indicators

Social foundation	Illustrative indicators	Percentage	Year*
Food security	Malnutrition among children < 5 years	22%	2018
Income	Population under poverty line <$1.90/day	10%	2019
Water and sanitation	Population with no access to clean drinking water	11%	2012
	Population with no access to sanitation	35%	2012
Health	Population with no access to essential healthcare	50%	2017
Education	Children who do not attend primary education	72 mln	2014
	Adult illiteracy	759 mln	2014
Energy	Population with no access to electricity	13%	2016
	Population with no access to clean cooking facilities	36%	2019
Gender equality	Difference in labour market participation between women (57%) and men in paid work (78%)	23%	2020
	Representation of women vs. men in national parliaments	25%	2020
Social equality	Population under median income in countries with Gini>0.35	33%	1995-2009
Political voice	E.g., population in countries with no political freedom or participation	To be specified	
Work	E.g., population with no access to decent work	To be specified	
Resilience	Population under multi-dimensional poverty line	To be specified	

* WHO (2018; 2017); World Bank (2020); CDC (2012); Humanium (2019); Panos et al. (2016); IEA (2019); WEF (2020) and Raworth (2012)
Source: indicators from Raworth 2012; figures updated

the ability of the ecological processes in question to recover, with disastrous consequences. Compassion for the poorest in society can be defended from an ethical and moral standpoint, and yet there is also an economic interest in countering extreme inequality (see Chapter 7). The same appeal to moral behaviour is increasingly being made in relation to nature, nature conservation and nature restoration, although less importance has been attached thus far to this morality than when it concerns our fellow human beings. The awareness that maintaining these ecological processes is vitally important to everyone is growing rapidly, however, and already leading to demonstrable changes in behaviour. In part thanks to the individual campaigning of the young Swedish schoolgirl Greta Thunberg, Swedes are increasingly experiencing 'flight shame' and 'climate anxiety' (Fransen, in *Trouw*, 2019), and these phenomena are spreading to other countries in the world. According to climate scientists, however, behavioural change is not fast and far-reaching enough. With some exceptions, citizens, businesses and governments are still failing to engage with the sustainability problem. The places and times at which social inequality and environmental problems become manifest can differ within the duration of a human lifetime, which also affects the perceived need to intervene. Opportunities are created when responsible sustainable behaviour becomes part of our moral sphere, whereby people start to tackle one other about their environmentally 'immoral' behaviour. This is ultimately a subjective value judgement, which can indeed play a determining role when weighing up economic choices.

Natural resource discounting

As long as economic growth is considered the most important objective and benchmark of progress, we will not succeed in making the transition to a sustainable economy. We therefore need new benchmarks (see Chapter 9), of which sustainability is one of the most important. In recent decades, economic growth has accelerated in newly emerging economies such as India, China, Russia and Brazil, but such growth is not automatically sustainable. By contrast, Colombia is an emerging economy that has ascribed a relatively high level of importance to the transition to a sustainable economy. We thus see emerging economies making very different choices about the quality of the economic growth they are pursuing. The old model, based on natural resource extraction, is not necessarily the chosen path to growth.

At the beginning of this chapter, sustainability was clearly defined as an economic development that reduces environmental pressure on nature. Sustainability is not an absolute, measurable concept, however; it is a spectrum. A certain type of production process, for example, may reduce environmental pressure, for instance by using wind energy, but wind energy also emits CO_2 and thus still puts pressure on the environment (although much less pressure). In other words, sustainability is by no means a black-and-white issue. With the aid of the three-dimensional WEM (Table 2 and Figure 5) and Table 8, we can trace the extent to which different economic agents make use of natural resources in the form of ecosystem services, in different economic processes. When economic agents use more natural resources and spaces than they invest in nature, for example by conserving nature or planting new trees, the group of agents in question overshoot the system. When less is used than is invested (in time or resources) in restoration and accretion, the agents concerned find themselves in the safe part of the sustainability spectrum.

The 'discounting' of economic activities involving nature takes place by means of production, consumption, redistribution and co-creation. In a general sense, I understand natural resource discounting to mean *'the method of current valuation in order to at least maintain future value'*. Based on this comparison, nature regeneration (restoration) should take place in order to counter future scarcity or depletion. Due to the ever more intensive use of natural resources, however, the opposite – degeneration – is happening. As Raworth (2017) argues, there is an urgent need for resource regeneration in order to counter irreversible damage to ecosystems, and loss of biodiversity and landscapes. By

Figure 13   The regenerative economy

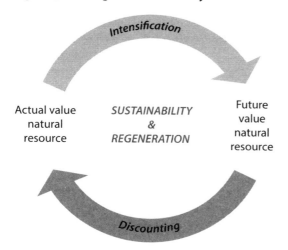

transitioning to a sustainable economy, the degree of intensification of the use of natural resources and space can be reduced,
so that we can actually speak of a 'regenerative economy' (see
also Figure 13). A regenerative economy is not only sustainable
(reduction of environmental pressure on nature), but also *focused
on the long-term qualitative restoration of nature'*.

Based on the WEM (Table 2, Chapter 5) and the dominant
allocation mechanisms in Figure 4 (Chapter 4), we can identify the
following analytical starting points for assessing sustainability
in the form of economic agents, processes and mechanisms, and
the influence they have on nature; see Table 8. When natural
resource discounting works out badly for nature, the degeneration
of natural resources will take place; when discounting has a
positive effect, regeneration will take place.

For each economic group of agents, natural resource discounting can be expressed in the following series of vector
equations (consisting of economic relations). These show how
many ecosystem services are used in a year compared to what
is added through natural recovery ('accretion') or the expansion
of natural space, which social relations are involved, and which

Table 8 Assessing sustainability: agents, processes and mechanisms

Sustainability of agents in relation to nature	Sustainability of economic processes	Sustainability of allocation mechanisms
Individuals		Reciprocity and support
Households	Consumption	Reciprocity and support
Firms and businesses	Production	Market exchange
Social groups and communities	Redistribution Co-creation	Reciprocity and support
Governments		Redistribution
Rest of the world		Market exchange
Hybrid partnerships		All mechanisms
⮡ **Nature**	⮡ **Discounting**	⮡ **De/regeneration**

subjective values are attached to this. Ultimately, these relations can be positive (regeneration), in equilibrium (preservation) or negative (degeneration):

Individuals:
$$(I_n): F_n\{M_i \cap R_i \cap S_i\} <=> (N_i):$$
$$F_i\{M_n \cap R_n \cap S_n\} \tag{E.01}$$

Households:
$$(H_n): F_n\{M_h \cap R_h \cap S_h\} <=> (N_h):$$
$$F_h\{M_n \cap R_n \cap S_n\} \tag{E.02}$$

Firms:
$$(F_n): F_n\{M_f \cap R_f \cap S_f\} <=> (N_f):$$
$$F_f\{M_n \cap R_f \cap S_f\} \tag{E.03}$$

Social groups/ communities:
$$(C_n): F_n\{M_c \cap R_c \cap S_c\} <=> (N_c):$$
$$F_c\{M_n \cap R_n \cap S_n\} \tag{E.04}$$

Governments:
$$(G_n): F_n\{M_g \cap R_g \cap S_g\} <=> (N_g):$$
$$F_g\{M_n \cap R_n \cap S_n\} \tag{E.05}$$

Rest of the world:
$$(W_n): F_n\{M_w \cap R_w \cap S_w\} <=> (N_w):$$
$$F_w\{M_n \cap R_n \cap S_n\} \tag{E.06}$$

The vector equations above are an abstract representation of human-economic-nature relations and require further specification and development, which can differ according to the economy, sector and economic activity. They can be linked to other quantifiable and qualitative measures and indicators, to facilitate interpretation and monitoring over time (see further Chapter 9). What is important to note here is that in the current system, the link to the SNA can only be made via quantifiable relations (as explained in Chapter 6, Figure 9), and the discounting will therefore need to be quantifiable. The material dimension of the wellbeing matrix (*WEM₁*) could provide the starting point for quantification. This would mean measuring the use of ecosystem services in terms of quantities, measures of space, or (imposed) monetary values. The equations above would then initially be simplified into the following series of material vector equations:

Individuals: $$(I_n): F_n\{M_i\} <=> (N_i): F_i\{M_n\} \qquad (E.07)$$

Households: $$(H_n): F_n\{M_h\} <=> (N_h): F_h\{M_n\} \qquad (E.08)$$

Firms: $$(F_n): F_n\{M_f\} <=> (N_f): F_f\{M_n\} \qquad (E.09)$$

Social groups/
communities: $$(C_n): F_n\{M_c\} <=> (N_c): F_c\{M_n\} \qquad (E.10)$$

Governments: $$(G_n): F_n\{M_g\} <=> (N_g): F_g\{M_n\} \qquad (E.11)$$

Rest of the world: $$(W_n): F_n\{M_w\} <=> (N_w): F_w\{M_n\} \qquad (E.12)$$

However, this does not yet measure most of the natural resources and space that we use for our economic activities. In order to define the value of nature in more detail, it needs to be operationalized further. In the ecological economy, we generally make two kinds of distinctions between the various functions that nature fulfils for human wellbeing.

First, the distinction between:
(i)   ecosystem services, which have a direct effect on the well-being of people and animals;
(ii) biodiversity, which has a direct and indirect effect on wellbeing and is important for the delivery of ecosystem services at present and in the future; and
(iii) landscapes, which also have a direct and indirect effect on wellbeing, based on aesthetic, cultural, spiritual or intellectual values.

Second, the distinction between different kinds of ecosystem services, in terms of:
(i.1) intermediary ecosystem services; and
(i.2) final ecosystem services.

All final services have a direct and observable effect on wellbeing. Final services are ecosystem services that have a direct influence on wellbeing, because they fulfil a human need or priority. For this reason, they are also included in the WEM (Table 2, Chapter 5) under the heading 'Nature' (column and row 7). Within the final ecosystem services, the following services are distinguished:[44](i.2.1) production services (production of crops, fish, drinking water), (i.2.2) regulating services (in part) (protection against natural disasters), and (i.2.3) cultural services (recreation, spirituality).

In this process of operationalization, the challenges presented by definitions and categorization immediately become visible. For the SNA, it is important to have unambiguous definitions and categories between countries and over time, as these are essential for making comparisons. However, this brings us back to the discussion in Chapter 4 on 'What is Economics?' On the one hand, Wellbeing Economics proposes that we abandon 'system thinking'

44   I hereby follow the recommendation of the Netherlands Environmental Assessment Agency (NPBL), which makes this distinction between final ecosystem services in a policy memo on 'the discounting rate for nature' (NPBL, 2015, p. 10).

in economics, and instead see the economy as an institutionalized process; but on the other hand, and when push comes to shove, as soon as we want to map out the exchange between economic agents and nature, we find ourselves back at a fixed, regulated system such as the National Accounts. This system is also linked to regulations and legislation at the national, regional and global levels. Based on the new perspective introduced in this book, it is not immediately possible to adjust institutionalized economic planning models, but sketching out new frameworks, concepts and measures does allow us to reflect creatively and make new proposals. All of this implies that nature should no longer be seen as a closing entry on the balance sheet in economic decisions, but as a starting point. Nature should play a paramount role in every economic decision.

9 New indicators

In February 2008, the former French President Sarkozy assembled a committee, led by Joseph Stiglitz, Amartya Sen and Jean-Paul Fitoussi,[45] to chart the limits of GNP as a key indicator of economic progress and investigate the potential of plural indicators and measures.[46] Wellbeing Economics also proposes alternative indicators and measures[47] for gauging economic progress, on the grounds that this will help to guide and give content to policy, formulate objectives and limits, and monitor change. Whether the economy is 'doing well' is usually measured with core economic growth indicators, such as national income, output and spending. When an economy is growing, we tend to think that things are going well in a country. By contrast, when an economy shrinks, we are concerned about falling into a recession. Consumer confidence, as the rhetoric and media reports tell us, rises and falls with economic trends of growth and contraction. It is indeed true that economic growth ensures extra revenue, employment and new investment in an economy, which drives production and spending; this is indisputable. However, the above-mentioned rhetoric has been criticized in this book with regard to four key points:

(i) Economic growth tells us nothing about stability, distribution and sustainability.

(ii) More growth is not always better; what matters is the quality of growth.

45 Back in 1995, Amartya Sen was already involved in developing the Human Development Index (HDI) together with the economist Mahbub Ul Haq, on behalf of the UNDP. The HDI is a composite index consisting of three dimensions: income, education and health (life span). Each year, the UN ranks the world's countries according to their score on the HDI index. Since 2010, an HDI has also been in use that corrects for inequality.

46 See Stiglitz, Sen and Fitoussi 2008.

47 By 'measures', I mean indicators that contain a guideline or objective. By 'indicators', I mean numbers or ratios.

(iii) How people and perceive and experience economics is partly subjective.
(iv) Economic progress is ultimately about optimizing wellbeing, not maximizing individual welfare.

As this book proposes that we replace the one-sided focus on growth with a focus on optimizing wellbeing as the most important measure of economic progress, there is a need for new, supplementary indicators and measures. These can complement the indicators that are already in use. In this chapter, I shall make proposals regarding (i) the broadening of economic measures and indicators, (ii) social equality and distribution, (iii) sustainability, and (iv) subjective indicators, referring back to the three-dimensional WEM (Table 2, Chapter 5).

Broader economic indicators and measures

In addition to national income, output and expenditure, the core indicators of economic progress and success usually include indicators relating to employment, amount of money, price index (consumer and producer), consumer confidence, turnover in retail trade and the food industry, trade, the housing market and the stock market. From a Wellbeing Economics perspective, this list of core indicators is striking in three respects:
(1) All of these indicators relate to economic activities in the paid (and formal) economy involving consumers, producers and banks. Most concern macroeconomic growth – the higher the indicators score compared to the past, the better.
(2) There are only two indicators that (indirectly) tell us something about a qualitative aspect of economic growth, namely economic stability: employment and consumer confidence.
(3) With the exception of the subjective measure on consumer confidence, all of these indicators are based on monetary variables.

I propose that the current economic indicators and measuresbe broadened to include indicators on (i) economic stability, (ii) the unpaid economy, (iii) social (in)equality and distribution indicators, (iv) sustainability indicators, and (v) subjective indicators of material and relational wellbeing.[48] Such indicators are needed as input in national wellbeing indicators, which provide a more holistic picture of how well or badly an economy is performing.

Governments and agencies make their own decisions about which aspects/dimensions of wellbeing to include in multi-dimensional wellbeing indicators such as these. Some series of wellbeing indicators are already in circulation, including the Genuine Progress Indicator (which offsets the negative effects of environmental pressure); various Wellbeing Indexes (OECD and the statistics agencies of Australia, the Netherlands, etc.); the 'Inclusive Wealth Index' (UNESCO); the Gross National Happiness Index (Bhutan); the 'Better Life Index' (OECD); and the Gallup 'Global Wellbeing' index. Their use in socio-economic policy remains limited, however, perhaps with the exception of the government of Bhutan, which consistently justifies investment in cultural preservation using the Gross National Happiness Index. Governments and agencies make their own decisions in this regard.

Application in policy and practice is limited and challenged by the lack of any embedding in an epistemological approach and theoretical framework, such as 'Wellbeing Economics'. After all, a new index will not change the dominant economic narrative in itself. A further difficulty lurks in the methodology, particularly when subjective indicators are involved. With the aid of Likert scales, qualitative data on opinions and feelings can be transformed into numerical data. By using standardization methods between the different underlying scales of sub-indicators, these can then be consolidated into a composite index. There are many

48   As the difference between 'measures' and 'indicators' was already explained in footnote 47, for reasons of brevity, I henceforth use the term 'economic indicators' to refer to both.

more challenges here for statisticians trying to create a coherent, representative wellbeing index, an issue to which I shall return at the end of this chapter.

Re. (i) Economic stability
There are many existing economic indicators within the material dimension of wellbeing, most of which relate to market-related income and expenditure. At present, however, there are no indicators in circulation that measure income stability (or stability of expenditure), despite the fact that 'stability' is an important factor for economic wellbeing. First, a certain degree of economic stability is good for the economy and for the general wellbeing of people and nature, because it gives people a sense of confidence and security. People can in principle draw on this sense of confidence to make (more) purposeful economic decisions. It provides them with certain guidelines, on the basis of which they can make plans for the future. In my research on poverty, my respondents frequently defined 'poverty' as 'not having a plan'. Stability provides a foundation, allowing people to make plans about future wellbeing. 'Stability' does not mean 'standing still', but the absence of negative fluctuations in material wellbeing. Indicators of economic stability can be constructed from every other economic indicator available over time, based on absolute numbers or change formulas (mostly in terms of relative

percentage change: $\left[\frac{New - Old}{Old} * 100\% \right]$). For example, we can

calculate the stability of income and expenditure, including income from work, investments, interest, subsidies and taxes; but the stability of material possessions (durable property such as a house or a piece of land, savings, financial investments) can also be measured in this way. At times of crisis or economic adversity, the first things people are often forced to part with are their material possessions. These disinvestments are not directly visible in change of income, but are undoubtedly important for long-term wellbeing. A person's ability to send their children to college might be thrown into doubt, or there might be no more land available on which to grow crops next year.

From a wellbeing perspective, I therefore argue that we should develop and use stability indicators such as these in addition to standard growth indicators, so that we can chart and monitor the material wellbeing of different social groups more effectively.

Re. (ii) The unpaid economy
Second, I argue for a broader set of indicators that give us a better picture of the contributions and costs of the unpaid economy (by individuals, households and social groups and communities). Since the mid-1990s, significant work on domestic labour, care and volunteer work has been done by the UNDP, particularly by feminist economists, who have made proposals in relation to time indicators and value rates for measuring unpaid care and labour in the economy. The most recent statistics show that the total value of the unpaid economy worldwide is estimated at 49% of GNP on average (UNDP 2017). When we add up the number of paid and unpaid labour hours, we see that around the world women work an average of 2-3 hours more than men, and that they carry out 2.5 times more labour in the unpaid economy than men. The gap is wider in low-income countries, to the disadvantage of women. In addition, a persistent difference remains between what men and women are paid for doing the same work. On average, women earn 77 cents of every dollar earned by a man for doing the same work (UNDP 2017). The breakdown by gender is thus important for these indicators. This is why in row and column 1 of the WEM (Table 2, Chapter 5), individuals are distinguished from households (in row and column 2). Empirical analysis of these indicators has shown to date that the total amount of work done by women is structurally underestimated and undervalued. This not only leads to an imbalance in material and relational wellbeing between women and men, but it also steers macroeconomic investment more in the direction of the paid economy, instead of towards the unpaid economy, where, after all, 'fewer returns' are observed. This subsequently leads to

misconceptions about the real added value of the redistribution of unpaid labour, female labour participation and the trade-offs this entails, and minimalistic policies on compensation for maternity leave, childcare, and measures such as parental leave. All of this limits the opportunities for creating wellbeing for people in general and, in many countries and cultures, for women and girls in particular.

In addition, it is important systematically to chart the quantity and value of social and community work (voluntary work) at the macroeconomic level. Many people spend a number of hours each week doing unpaid voluntary work for associations, professional bodies, neighbourhoods, aid organizations and other agencies and initiatives. Individuals also organize themselves into social groups and communities that collectively carry out voluntary work (see Table 2, Chapter 5, row and column 4). For example, a neighbourhood association might decide collectively to maintain a neighbourhood's green spaces and playgrounds each year. For many people, this is a way of making a meaningful contribution to collective social wellbeing, in terms of aspects such as solidarity, social cohesion and support. It also contributes to the subjective wellbeing of the volunteers and 'recipients', because it makes them feel part of a group or community. The value of such forms of meaning-creation is subjective and difficult to measure, but the time (and resources) involved can be measured and used as an indirect indicator.

In Chapter 4, we explained the underlying relationship between the unpaid and paid economies. The two are interrelated and mutually dependent. If we want to know whether there have been changes to wellbeing, it is thus strange not to use any indicators at the macroeconomic level that tell us about the unpaid economy. By basing everything on the performance of the paid economy, we are blind to the added value of interactions with the unpaid economy. This is why I also propose a series of national indicators that express the value (in time units, use of physical and natural resources and space, and/or money) of unpaid domestic work, care work and voluntary work together.

The UNDP (2017) already uses a number of indicators for this, but they are not visible in all National Accounts or used actively when formulating policy. In addition, I propose a series of economic measures that indicate the degree of (dis)equilibrium between the distribution of unpaid and paid labour and its valuation, which can be used to guide socio-economic policy and interventions. This also allows us to investigate and understand the exchange between the paid and unpaid economies at the macroeconomic level, and to go beyond the microeconomic studies that mainly analyse the distribution of paid and unpaid work within and between households, but do not use this to draw aggregated conclusions about collective wellbeing in an economy.

Re. (iii) Social (in)equality and distribution indicators
In Chapter 5 of this book, I argued that more systematic attention should be paid in economic analysis to charting and investigating different forms of inequality in the three dimensions of wellbeing, with the aid of the diagonal in the layered WEM (Table 2, Chapter 5): interpersonal inequalities, between households, firms and businesses, social groups and communities, governments and countries.

There are already a number of important income inequality indicators relating to material wellbeing, including the Gini coefficient,[49] the Palma ratio[50] and the S80/S20 (proportion of the average equivalent income of the highest quintile compared to the lowest quintile). This latter indicator is also used by Eurostat as a measure of social inclusion (the degree to which everyone is able to participate in society). These indicators are usually based on income/expenditure and wealth. In principle, however, inequality indicators such as these can be developed to

49 The Gini coefficient measures total income inequality between all people in a population. In a general sense, the Gini coefficient can be used as an indicator of every type of distribution.
50 The Palma ratio is the income ratio between the richest 10% and poorest 40% of a population.

measure any variable distribution in a population, such as years of education, illness and health, nutrition, criminal convictions, hours worked (paid and unpaid) or leisure time, and so forth. From a wellbeing perspective, it is extremely important not only to consider inequality in terms of income/assets, but also indicators that tell us something about the distribution of other forms of material, relational and subjective wellbeing. Inequality indicators should also be gender-specific. This allows societies to measure how much of the total perceived inequality, for example in income or working hours, is explained by gender inequality or inequality affecting minority groups. Research should always consider the impact of gender (or other) inequality in aggregated inequality indicators, before socio-economic policies are developed to influence inequality in a general sense. This argument is not only driven by a sense of social justice, but also by efficiency considerations. When gender (or other) inequalities play a relatively large role in the total degree of inequality, this is where the greatest gains can be made.

Finally, I want to argue for the development and use of economic indicators that ascribe more relative weight to the circumstances of the very poorest (for example, by giving two or three times more weight to the lowest income groups in a poverty or inequality indicator). For them, a small change can make a greater difference (e.g., good nutrition and clean drinking water, a first bicycle), and the opposite is also true. A small change in the circumstances of the very wealthiest makes a smaller difference (e.g., a second home or a third car). The political philosopher John Rawls (1921-2002) made a case for indicators such as these in his pioneering book, *A Theory of Justice* (1971), because they could be used to guide redistributive policy. He had a vision of more social and economic justice in which the interests of the poorest were captured and made visible in economic indicators. According to Rawls, social and economic 'inequalities' in provisions and policy are justified when they lead to the greatest added value for the very poorest or most disadvantaged. His vision is at odds with individual utilitarianism, which instead measures value on the basis of the greatest contribution to the common good. Rawls believed this to be unfair, because the very poorest tend to lack the opportunity to make a (large) contribution to the common good. When the new Sustainable Development Goals were adopted globally on 1 January 2016, with the secondary goal of 'leaving no one behind', a new framework was created for making such trade-offs in policy and practice. After all, it had been established in 2015, in the wake of the Millennium Development Goals, that development interventions were failing to reach the very poorest, and that the latter often trail behind in processes of economic growth and development (UN 2016). Due to the complex interaction between social exclusion and self-exclusion, people in extreme poverty often fail to participate meaningfully in society (Altaf 2019). Extra effort and resources are needed to involve these people in the process of improving wellbeing. Representing the very poorest in economic indicators and statistics, such as those that Rawls had in mind, would make them more visible in politics and economics. The degree to which people succeed in creating wellbeing in all three dimensions (material, relational and subjective), and the extent to which this differs, could be the ultimate inequality indicator.

Re. (iv) Sustainability indicators

The embedding of 'nature' in the Wellbeing Economics Matrix gives us all the more reason to use robust indicators to make the contribution of, extraction of and pressure on natural resources visible in relation to wellbeing.

Whereas the nine planetary boundaries developed by Rockström and his team (2009) offer a clear framework of objective indicators about the state of our ecosystems relative to the economy, other sustainability indicators are also used to measure environmental pressure or energy consumption (e.g., carbon emissions and the ecological footprint). The coming decades will see the addition of dozens of new indicators that are expected to play an ever-greater role in determining socio-economic and geopolitical policy and private sector development. This can only be welcomed. We are gradually seeing the formulation and use of more specific sustainability indicators, for example with regard to various ecosystem services, energy consumption and different forms of environmental impact. This allows scientists and policymakers to observe trends over time and draw up guidelines and measures for a sustainable economy, and to enter into the public debate about the sustainability of international trade, agriculture, industry, services, technology and lifestyles. The following types of indicators are increasingly being used (or their use is being encouraged by the government) to make sustainability targets concrete and measurable: (i) biodiversity indicators, (ii) extraction standards, (iii) pollution standards and (iv) footprint per sector. To supplement these, I propose indicators relating to: (v) investments in nature, distinguishing between (a) nature conservation and (b) recovery.

Re. (i) Biodiversity indicators
Agreements have been made at the international level to protect and maintain biodiversity. These are contained in conventions such as the UN Convention on Biological Diversity (CBD) and EU guidelines. Between 1992 and 2020, for example, the Aichi Biodiversity Targets were gradually adopted by 150 countries.[51] In 2020, the post-2020 global biodiversity framework will be used to make the step towards the 2050 vision of 'Life in Harmony with Nature'. The countries that have signed this convention are obliged to protect and maintain variation in ecosystems, genes, and (native) species in their own countries as effectively as possible. As it is simply impossible to measure change across all species, a purposeful selection is sufficient. The most representative species is often chosen when monitoring the quality of ecosystems. On the one hand, there is a long list of biodiversity indicators that are characteristic of the quality of

---

51   The Aichi Biodiversity Targets were drawn up following the 1992 Earth Summit in Rio de Janeiro, and were eventually signed by 150 countries.

ecosystems (e.g., the quality of waterways, forest, and other landscapes) and the presence of species and genes. On the other hand, measures that are linked to policy are also formulated, such as the degree of awareness of the value of biodiversity and the steps that people can take to maintain and sustainably manage biodiversity (e.g., the biodiversity barometer or online interest shown in biodiversity). These cover both objective and subjective data. The nature of the measures change when the policy targets change. Finally, a distinction is made between generic and specific biodiversity indicators. An example of a generic indicator is 'trends in the use of natural resources'. Two specific indicators within this generic indicator are the ecological footprint and the quantity of material consumption. The 'ecological footprint' is a calculation of how much space on Earth is taken up by a person, company or sector. This 'space' is determined using a model that calculates the raw materials, energy and resource use associated with a certain lifestyle or production process. As the ecological footprint also measures carbon emissions, it is also seen as a pollution indicator. Biodiversity indicators can be included in row/column 7 'Nature' of the WEM (Table 2, Chapter 5). A rise in biodiversity contributes to a rise in wellbeing, and a fall in biodiversity results in less wellbeing, in the present or in the future.

Re. (ii) Extraction standards
Extraction standards are indicators that serve as guidelines for maintaining an equilibrium between the extraction of a raw material and existing reserves and needs. These are drawn up for a certain period, in the following generic form:

$\left(\dfrac{Extraction}{Reserve} * 100\% \right)$. For the extraction of fresh water, for

example, ground water reserves need to be monitored, as well as changes in related systems such as rainfall, evaporation, water supply and drainage, and socio-economic use. As soon as these other variables are included in the calculation of the correct extraction standard, this can be described as a 'model'. Extraction standards must therefore be adjusted continuously on the basis of other influencing variables, such as climatological and socio-economic change. When it was established in 2019 that the increasing earthquakes in the Province of Groningen in the northern Netherlands, and corresponding damage to homes and security threats, had been caused by the gas extraction industry, extraction standards were swiftly revised downwards. It is expected that gas extraction in Groningen will be brought to a complete halt in 2022. In the meantime, the Dutch government, which earned significant revenues from gas extraction, is undertaking a thorough search for other (sustainable) energy sources, such as biomass, because it wants to avoid dependency on imported gas. The costs of the extraction process form part of the standard cost-benefit analysis by companies and organizations in the raw materials industry. The costs of extraction for nature itself, however, in terms of pollution or use of natural resources, are not calculated. Nature should be protected by means of standards and investments in sustainable and circular use. This possible in the WEM (Table 2, Chapter 5), by including this as a cost item for all economic agents in row/column 7 on 'Nature'.

Re. (iii) Pollution standards
Perhaps the best-known pollution standard is the CO_2 standard, measured in terms of the amount of carbon dioxide in the atmosphere. The heat that the Earth receives from the sun is radiated outwards into space. It is partly absorbed by the amount of carbon dioxide in the atmosphere. The more CO_2 there is the atmosphere, the less heat from the sun is radiated out into space. This is known as the greenhouse effect, whereby the Earth becomes warmer. There are several CO_2 standards in circulation as pollution standards, and a distinction is usually made between direct and indirect carbon emissions. Direct carbon emissions occur when energy is consumed by businesses, consumers and other users. Indirect carbon emissions occur as a result of the clothes we wear, the things we use and the food we eat. The average Dutch

household directly emits 8 tons of CO_2 each year, and indirectly emits 12.5 tons. Based on the calculations by Rockström (2009), 350 ppm (parts per million) is currently used as a global approximate safe limit for the concentration of CO_2 in the atmosphere. Below this limit, global warming will remain manageable (below 2 degrees Celsius). The challenge is for all energy users to reach this target collectively. If the failure of companies to report their carbon emissions is not accompanied by sanctions, there will be little compulsion to reduce emissions. The same is true for households; as of yet, there is no form of sanction if things get out of hand. To date, much government policy has focused on guiding people in the direction of the energy transition on a voluntary basis. Tough aims and measures could follow, such as setting a deadline for disconnecting all households from the natural gas network. In addition to carbon emissions, there are also additional pollution standards, such as those for water or soil. Most of these measure concentrations of volatile carbons, oil, asbestos, heavy metals, dioxins and cyanides that are toxic for nutrients and minerals in water and soil, as well as for plants, animals and humans. Pollution can be included as a cost item in the WEM (Table 2, Chapter 5), in row/column 7 on 'Nature', by basing this on the costs of preventing or cleaning up pollution.

Re. (iv) Investing in nature
In the transition to a sustainable economy, societies, governments and businesses are becoming increasingly aware of the importance of nature for our wellbeing and the wellbeing of future generations. We only have one Earth. The intention can hardly be to ruin it, and to pour all our resources into finding an alternative planet that is capable of sustaining life. From an economic perspective, it is therefore extremely important to invest in nature conservation and restoration. For this purpose, Kate Raworth uses the Doughnut Economy (Figure 12) as a vision of an economy that is no longer focused on consumption (and the corresponding pollution and depletion of nature), but on regeneration and distribution. Thus, from this perspective and

from a Wellbeing Economics perspective, spending on nature conservation and recovery/reinforcement is not a cost item, but an investment in wellbeing. After all, these 'green investments' ultimately provide something, too: biodiversity, natural resources, clean air, water and green space. The difficulty lies in determining their economic value. This should not be seen as the 'marketization' of nature, but as a way of making it visible in economic models and planning. There are various methods for doing this: (i) an indirect market value is calculated on the basis of what nature 'delivers' to leisure-seekers who contribute to the economy in a region, (ii) a price is attached to having access to nature, based on what people are prepared to pay, (iii) it is jointly determined what it is worth to a community to maintain a particular natural area, landscape or animal species, as is currently the case for cultural heritage. When investments in nature conservation and recovery/reinforcement are viewed as economically sound, they will play a much more important role in economic planning models and scenario sketches, rather than being an expensive cost item or closing entry on a balance sheet. This is why 'Nature' is a key 'agent' in the Wellbeing Economics Matrix and is no longer invisible, as it was in earlier social accounting matrices (SAMs; see background discussion about this in Chapter 5). Given that the WEM forms the foundation of all further economic analysis and planning, at the very least, including it in its basis will secure its further use in economic models and calculations. It is this that makes 'Wellbeing Economics' a robust economic vision that goes far beyond the replacement of GNP with a wellbeing indicator. With the aid of a Wellbeing Economics Matrix (WEM) as a theoretical starting point, I come to the following generic formulation of a three-dimensional wellbeing index:

$$Wellbeing = \frac{\sum_{i,j}^{n} \left(M_{i,j} + R_{i,j} + S_{i,j} \right)}{3} \tag{E.13}$$

Whereby M stands for a set of indicators of material wellbeing, R stands for a set of indicators of relational wellbeing, S stands for a set of indicators of subjective wellbeing, and i and j for agent i in dimension j, respectively. Within each dimension, we need to select indicators that are together considered to be representative of a society's material, socio-relational and subjective wellbeing. Such an index can also be drawn up for lower scale-levels, however, such as 'Wellbeing in the City', and monitored over time. For use in policymaking, the 'Wellbeing Index' can be set up as a 'dashboard', with buttons (indicators) that can alternately be turned on and off. There will be different wellbeing priorities at different scale levels, but it is important not to lose sight of them altogether – hence the 'dashboard'. A generic (not filled-in) example is shown in Figure 14. A dark area indicates that this button (indicator) has been turned off temporarily, because it is not currently a priority. The specific context determines the choice of indicators in each dimension. It is important to note, however, that these indicators are integrally linked to one other.

Once a composite wellbeing index such as this has been developed, embedded in 'Wellbeing Economics', economic analysts and planning agencies will be able to monitor progress or decline and trace it back to income and expenditure, equalities and inequalities, and the use and valuation of nature in the WEM (Table 2, Chapter 5). Although policy decisions are always political, they can be rooted in and designed on the basis of a robust framework. Rather than steering primarily on the basis of economic growth and only considering social equality and nature conservation *post facto*, *ex ante* investment is logical here, because it contributes to individual and collective wellbeing. There is still no guarantee, though, that everyone will be able to optimize their wellbeing. For this purpose, representation, participation and voice in policy decisions will need to be organized in an inclusive fashion, with representation for social minorities. What is more, in order to find the requisite political and executive capacity and be strategically deployable, the composite wellbeing index should be linked to policy domains and instruments. Otherwise, an index such as this will lack embeddedness. Finally, I wish to underline once again that 'Wellbeing' tells us about processes and outcomes, and in this

Figure 14   Generic dashboard for the Wellbeing Economy

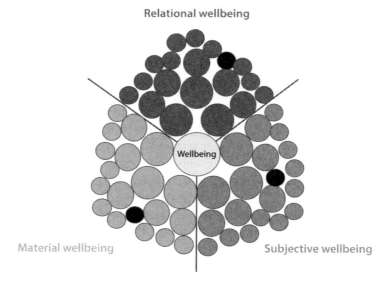

Relational wellbeing

Wellbeing

Material wellbeing   Subjective wellbeing

sense, it can change over time and between different contexts. The prioritization of indicators changes over time when certain objectives have been reached, or when needs change. Opinions and feelings play a major role when setting priorities, which can lead to certain rankings of wellbeing indicators. This is another way in which a Wellbeing Index represents subjective values.

10   Looking ahead

In the previous chapters, I have attempted to offer the reader an alternative vision of economics; a vision that focuses on human wellbeing and nature, rather than money and possessions. In my view, in order to be able to respond adequately to pressing global questions about inequality, sustainability and globalization, we need this holistic vision to achieve the transition to a sustainable and (more) social economy. Economic growth promotes wellbeing, but there are also limits to growth, and this makes critical research essential. It is my personal conviction that monistic theories on the market economy are no longer sufficient. They are blind to the complex economic processes and changes in our society and the interactions between humans and nature, with the implication that we fail to anticipate threats, as well as the unexpected events associated with them, in good time.

With this book, I am keen to invite economists and non-economists to contribute to the further development of 'Wellbeing Economics'. Although I have tried to capture the full spectrum of economic ontology, epistemology and theory in a methodology, I am aware that my description is far from complete. Work thus remains to be done. As axioms in science,[52] and thus also in economic science, can only exist *if they are shared by people*, I also invite non-economists to join me in fleshing out this initial framework of Wellbeing Economics.

I am also making an appeal to economic education. In both secondary and higher education, I would advocate the redrafting of economic teaching material and the training of lecturers based on a broader vision of economics, using new textbooks.[53] Subjects

---

52 Axiom = a foundation or claim accepted as a basic principle, which characterizes a theory.

53 Changing economic textbooks is not particularly straightforward, because the practice of economics is closely bound up with economic theories (see also: David Colander's 2015 article on 'Why economics textbooks should, but don't,

such as sustainable economics, inequality, climate change, social and political institutions and wellbeing, as well as qualitative methods and skills (in addition to quantitative ones), should be high on the agenda in economic education. The discipline of economics needs young thinkers who can ask critical questions and make creative contributions to 'Wellbeing Economics' in the form of new concepts, theories, indicators and methodological development. When it comes to methods and techniques, the discipline should be more open to qualitative methodologies, such as narrative, descriptive and (historical) process analysis. These should be much more complementary to the quantitative methods and techniques that currently dominate economic education and economic science as a whole. I personally derive much pleasure and satisfaction from quantitative analysis; economics offers a wonderful range of quantitative methods and techniques, and there is nothing more satisfying than doing an analysis and showing that it agrees with the model you had in mind. At the same time, I am aware of the limits of quantitative analysis; it does not allow me to answer the underlying 'how' and 'why' questions, or get a grip on an economic phenomenon in the context of a specific time or place. In fact, the economic models that are used on a large scale to make important financial decisions, for example, also pose a risk, due to the way in which they can be used by a small group of experts, and the importance that is simultaneously attached to them in economic analysis.

Finally, because I am at heart an economist and wish to enthuse others about economic science, I want to encourage my colleagues in the discipline to keep debating and working on research with colleagues from the other social sciences, as well as from the natural and behavioural sciences. As economists, we have a lot to offer: knowledge about how people make complex trade-offs when making economic decisions, how people pursue wellbeing, what the consequences of economic policy are for

and won't, change', in the *European Journal of Economics and Economic Policies: Intervention*, 12(2), 229-235.

society and the natural world, and so forth. On the other hand, our colleagues' knowledge of culture, power, space, history and the spirit of the age helps us to formulate questions and understand economics better. I am convinced that such interactions make us better economists, and increase our discipline's relevance to the everyday experience and practice of economics.

Bibliography

Akerlof, G., 'The Market for "Lemons": Quality Uncertainty and the Market Mechanism', *Quarterly Journal of Economics*, 84 (1970), pp. 235-251.

Altaf, A., *The Many Hidden Faces of Extreme Poverty. Inclusion and Exclusion of Extreme Poor People in Development Interventions in Bangladesh, Benin and Ethiopia* (Leiden: African Studies Centre, Leiden University, 2019).

Becker, G., *A Treatise on the Family* (Cambridge MA: Harvard University Press, 1981).

Bowles, S. and H. Gintis, *A Cooperative Species: Human Reciprocity and Its Evolution* (Princeton: Princeton University Press, 2013).

CDC, 'Global Water, Sanitation and Hygiene Fact Sheet Based on 2012 Data' (Centers for Disease Control and Prevention, 2019). Accessed 17 December 2019: https://www.cdc.gov/healthywater/global/wash_statistics.html.

Centraal Bureau voor de Statistiek [Statistics Netherlands], 'CBS Activiteiten op het gebied van brede welvaart en duurzaamheid, CBS Nota 210953' (The Hague: CBS, 2015). Accessed 23 February 2019: https://www.cbs.nl/nl-nl/achtergrond/2016/16/cbs-nota-brede-welvaart-en-duurzaamheid

Centraal Bureau voor de Statistiek [Statistics Netherlands], Monitor Brede Welvaart en de SDGs 2019' (The Hague: CBS, 2019). Accessed 15 March 2020: https://www.cbs.nl/nl-nl/publicatie/2019/20/monitor-brede-welvaart-sdg-s-2019

Chang, H.-Y., *Bad Samaritans: The Myth of Free Trade and the Secret History of Capitalism* (New York: Bloomsbury Press, 2007).

Coats, A.W., 'The Current "Crisis" in Economics in Historical Perspective', *Nebraska Journal of Economics and Business*, 16 (1976), pp. 3-16.

Colander, D., 'Why Economics Textbooks Should, but Don't, and Won't, Change', *European Journal of Economics and Economic Policies: Intervention*, 12 (2015), pp. 229-235.

Cooley, C., 'Political Economy and Social Process', *Journal of Political Economy*, 26 (1918), pp. 366-374.

Costanza, R., E. Caniglia, L. Fioramonti, I. Kubiszewski., H. Lewis, H. Lovins, ... and K.V. Ragnarsdóttir, 'Towards a Sustainable Wellbeing Economy', *Solut J*, 9 (2018).

Coyle, D., *The Economics of Enough. How to Run the Economy as if the Future Matters* (Princeton: Princeton University Press, 2011).

Degrowth: A Vocabulary for a New Era, ed. by D'Alisa, G., F. Demaria and G. Kallis (New York: Routledge, 2014).

Dasgupta, P., 'Nature and the economy', *Journal of Applied Ecology*, 44 (2007), pp. 475-487.

Davis, J.B., *The Theory of the Individual in Economics: Identity and Value* (New York: Routledge, 2003).

Eisler, R., *The Real Wealth of Nations: Creating a Caring Economy* (Oakland, C.A.): Berrett-Koehler Publishers Inc., 2007).

Esping-Andersen, G., *The Three Worlds of Welfare Capitalism* (Cambridge: Polity Press, 1990).

Fine, B., 'Vicissitudes of Economics Imperialism', *Review of Social Economy*, 66 (2008), pp. 235-340.

Fine, B., *Women's Employment and the Capitalist Family* (New York: Routledge, 2010).

Folbre, N., *Who Pays for the Kids? Gender and the Structure of Constraints* (London: Routledge, 1993).

Foucault, M., *The History of Sexuality* (New York: Random House, 1978).

Foucault, M., 'The Subject and Power', *Critical Theory*, 8 (1981), pp. 777-795.

Fransen, A.G., 'Zweden raken in de ban van vliegschaamte en klimaatangst', *Trouw*, 1 March 2019: https://www.trouw.nl/nieuws/de-zweden-raken-in-de-ban-van-vliegschaamte-en-klimaatangst~b9ef07e8/.

Fullbrook, E., *Ontology and Economics. Tony Lawson and his Critics* (London: Routledge, 2009).

Golding, I., 'Navigating our Global Future', TED Talk in 2009. Accessed 13 October 2019: http://blog.ted.com/2009/10/23/navigating_our/.

Gough, I. and J.A. McGregor, *Wellbeing in Developing Countries. From Theory to Practice* (Cambridge: Cambridge University Press, 2007).

Granovetter, M., *Society and Economy: Framework and Principles* (Cambridge MA: Kelknap Press, Harvard University Press, 2017).

Heertje, A., *Echte Economie. Een verhandeling over schaarste en welvaart en over het geloof in leermeesters en lerne* (Nijmegen: Valkhof Pers, 2006).

Humanium, 'Right to Education. Situation around the World' (Geneva: Humanium, 2019). Accessed 3 March 2020: https://www.humanium.org/en/right-to-education/.

IEA, 'Shaping a Secure and Sustainable Energy Future for All' (Paris: International Energy Agency, 2019). Accessed 3 March 2020: https://www.iea.org/reports/sdg7-data-and-projections/access-to-clean-cooking.

International Student Initiative for Pluralism in Economics, *Open Letter 2014-2015*. Accessed 6 February 2018: http://www.isipe.net/open-letter/.

Kahneman, D. and A. Tversky, 'Prospect theory: An Analysis of Decision Under Risk', *Econometrica*, 47 (1979), pp. 263-291.

Kuiper, E., *The Most Valuable of All Capital. A Gender Reading of Economic Texts* (Amsterdam: Thela Thesis, 2001).

Lawson, T., *Economics and Reality* (London: Routledge, 1997).

Lawson, T., *Reorienting Economics* (London: Routledge, 2003).

Lawson, T., *Essays on the Nature and State of Modern Economics* (London: Routledge, 2015).

Lee, F., *A History of Heterodox Economics. Challenging the Mainstream in the 20th Century* (London: Routledge, 2010).

Lindbeck, A., *The Political Economy of the New Left* (New York: Harper and Row, 1971).

Lutz, M., *Economics for the Common Good: Two Centuries of Economic Thought in the Humanist Tradition* (London: Routledge, 1999).

McGregor, J.A., 'Researching Wellbeing: Communicating between the Needs of Policy Makers and the Needs of People', *Global Social Policy*, 4 (2004), pp. 337-358.

McGregor, J.A. 'Researching Human Wellbeing: From Concepts to Methodology', in *Wellbeing in Developing Countries: From Theory to Research*, ed. by I. Gough and J.A. McGregor (Cambridge: Cambridge University Press, 2007).

McGregor, J.A. and N.R.M Pouw, 'Towards an Economics of Wellbeing', *Cambridge Journal of Economics*, 41 (2016), pp. 1123-1143.

Meadows, D.H., J. Randers and W.W. Behrens III, *The Limits to Growth: A Report to the Club of Rome* (Rome, 1972).

Milanovic, B., *Global Inequality. A New Approach for the Age of Globalization* (Belknap Press, Harvard University Press, 2016).

NPBL, 'De Discontovoet voor Natuur. De relatieve prijsstijging voor ecosysteemdiensten', PBL Policy Brief (The Hague: Nederlands Planbureau voor de Leefomgeving, 2015).

Panos, E., M. Densing, and K. Volkart, 'Access to Electricity in the World Energy Council's Global Energy Scenarios: An Outlook for Developing Regions until 2030', *Energy Strategy Reviews*, 9 (2016), pp. 28-49.

Piketty, T., *Le Capital au XXIme ciècle* (Paris: Editions de Seuille, 2014).

Polanyi, K., *The Great Transformation* (Boston MA: Beacon Press, 1944).

Pouw, N.R.M., 'When Growth is Empty. Towards an Inclusive Economics', *The Broker,* 25 (June/July 2011), pp. 4-8.

Pouw, N.R.M. and J.A. McGregor, 'An Economics of Wellbeing. What Would Economics Look Like if it were Focused on Human Wellbeing?' *IDS Working Paper 436*, (Sussex: Institute of Development Studies, 2014).

Pouw, N.R.M. and J. Gupta, 'Inclusive Development in Search of Political Will', (The Hague: INCLUDE Knowledge Platform, 2015). Accessed 29 January 2018: https://includeplatform.net/contribution/inclusive-development-search-political-will/.

Pouw, N.R.M., *Introduction to Gender and Wellbeing in Microeconomics* (London and New York: Routledge, 2017).

Putnam, R., 'Social Capital: Measurement and Consequences', *Canadian Journal of Policy Research*, 2 (2001), pp. 41-51.

Pyatt, G. and E. Thorbecke, *Planning Techniques for a Better Future* (Geneva: International Labour Office, 1976).

Rawls, J., *A Theory of Justice* (Harvard: Cambridge Press, 1971).

Raworth, K., 'A Safe and Just Space for Humanity. Can We Live Within the Doughnut?' *Oxfam Discussion Papers* (London: Oxfam, 2012).

Raworth, K., *Doughnut Economics: Seven Ways to Think Like a 21st-century Economist* (London: Chelsea Green Publishing, 2017).

Rijksoverheid Nederland, 'Circulaire Economie 2019'. Accessed 7 February 2020: https://www.rijksoverheid.nl/onderwerpen/circulaire-economie/alle-grondstoffen-hergebruiken.

Rockström, J., W. Steffen, K. Noone, Å. Persson, F.S. Chapin, E.F. Lambin, ... and B. Nykvist, 'A Safe Operating Space for Humanity', *Nature*, 461 (2009), pp. 472-475.

Sen, A.K., 'Rational Fools: A Critique of the Behavioral Foundations of Economic Theory', *Philosophy and Public Affairs,* 6 (1977), pp. 317-344.

Sen, A.K., 'Positional Objectivity', *Philosophy and Public Affairs,* 22 (1993), pp. 126-145.

Sen, A.K., *Development as Freedom* (New York: Alfred A. Knop, 1999).

Sen, A.K., *The Idea of Justice* (Harvard University Press and London: Allen Lane, 2009).

Simon, H., *Models of Man, Social and Rational: Mathematical Essays on Rational Human Behavior in a Social Setting* (New York: Wiley, 1957).

Staveren, I. van, *The Values of Economics. An Aristotelian Perspective* (New York: Routledge, 2001).

Stiglitz, J., A.K. Sen and J.P. Fitoussi, 'Measuring Economic Performance and Social Progress' (Paris: Report by the Commission on the Measurement of Economic Performance and Social Progress, 2009).

Szreter, S., 'The State of Social Capital: Bringing Back in Power, Politics, and History', *Theory and Society,* 31 (2002), pp. 573-621.

Tilly, C., *Durable Inequality* (University of California Press, 1998).

Tverksy, A. and D. Kahnemann, 'Judgment Under Uncertainty: Heuristics and Biases', *Science,* 185 (1974), pp. 1124-1131.

Tverksy, A. and D. Kahnemann, 'The Framing of Decisions and the Psychology of Choice', *Science,* 211 (1981), pp. 453-458.

Tverksy, A. and D. Kahnemann, 'Advances in Prospect Theory: Cumulative Representation of Uncertainty', *Journal of Risk and Uncertainty,* 5 (1992), pp. 297-323.

UN, 'The Sustainable Development Goals Report' (New York: United Nations, 2016).

UNDP, 'Women's Economic Empowerment in the Changing World of Work', Report of the Secretary-General, E/CN6/2-17/3 (New York: United Nations Development Programme, 2017).

WeD, 'ESRC Research Statement on Wellbeing', Wellbeing in Development Research Group (Sussex: University of Bath, 2007). Accessed 10 December 2017: http://www.welldev.org.uk/research/aims.htm.

WEF, 'Global Risks Report 2020' (Davos: World Economic Forum, 2020).

WEF, 'Global Gender Gap Report 2020' (Davos: World Economic Forum, 2020).

WHO, 'Global Nutrition Report 2018', (Geneva: World Health Organization, 2018). Accessed 6 December 2019: https://www.who.int/nutrition/globalnutritionreport/en/.

WHO, 'Half the world lacks access to essential health services' (Geneva: World Health Organization, 2017). Accessed 6 December 2019: https://www.who.int/news-room/detail/13-12-2017-world-bank-and-who-half-the-world-lacks-access-to-essential-health-services-100-million-still-pushed-into-extreme-poverty-because-of-health-expenses.

Wilkinson, R.G. and K. Pickett, *The Spirit Level: Why More Equal Societies Almost Always Do Better* (London: Allen Lane, 2009).

World Bank, 'Understanding Poverty' (Washington D.C.: World Bank, 2019). Accessed 5 September 2019: https://www.worldbank.org/en/topic/poverty/overview.

About the author

Nicky Pouw is an associate professor at the University of Amsterdam, where she works for the multi-disciplinary Governance for Inclusive Development (GID) research programme at the Faculty of Social and Behavioural Sciences. She researches human wellbeing in the context of international and local social, economic and political development, particularly in global locations where people face poverty, discrimination or marginalization. The world's poorest are always a focus of her research. Her work mainly covers African countries, but she also does research in countries beyond Africa, including Guatemala, Indonesia, Sri Lanka and the Netherlands. In addition, she is active in the debate about inclusive and sustainable development from a global perspective. This gives her a broad and comparative economic perspective on issues such as poverty, inequality, wellbeing, gender, food security, sustainability, entrepreneurship and inclusive global development. In her applied research projects on social security systems, inclusive food systems and the social-economic exclusion of vulnerable youth, she also works on the epistemology of economic thought and economic knowledge. She is the author and co-publisher of *Introduction to Gender and Wellbeing in Microeconomics* (2017), *Local Governance and Poverty in Developing Nations* (2012) and *The Wellbeing of Women in Entrepreneurship: A Global Perspective* (2019), published by Routledge. She also publishes frequently in scholarly journals on social, political and economic development, and she has guest-edited three special issues on Inclusive Development and Inclusive Entrepreneurship for Food Security (*European Journal of Development Research*, 2015; *Current Opinion in Environmental Sustainability*, 2017, with Joyeeta Gupta; and *Current Opinion in Environmental Sustainability,* 2019, with Simon Bush and Ellen Mangnus). She directs a number of international research programmes in Africa and elsewhere, and gives lectures and talks on inclusive development and wellbeing economics. She is the chair of the board of *The Broker*, co-leader of the EADI's Inclusive Development working group, and is a member of Statistics Netherlands' working group on 'Measuring New Phenomena in Economics'. Finally, she is managing editor of the scholarly journal *International Environmental Agreements: Politics, Law and Economics*, published by Springer.

Index